Charles R. Anderson, MLS

Puzzles and Essays
from "The Exchange"
Tricky Reference Questions

Pre-publication
REVIEWS,
COMMENTARIES,
EVALUATIONS . . .

"'The Exchange' column in RQ is a beloved institution among librarians. Over the years, numerous jewels of reference information have been presented in its pages. Charles Anderson has splendidly continued the tradition of 'The Exchange,' editing it since 1984.

This book presents many of the most interesting reference questions and answers from the column. The entries on 'the success quotation,' 'words ending in –gry,' 'books without the letter e,' 'the origins of tiddlywinks,' and 'the origins of the peace symbol' are each alone worth the price of the book. Anderson also prints eight of his own essays on reference librarianship, exploring such timely issues as universal access and the future of the reference librarian profession."

Fred R. Shapiro, MSLS, JD
Associate Librarian for Collections
and Access and Lecturer
in Legal Research,
Yale Law School

"People ask the strangest questions and librarians answer them. Readers of *Puzzles and Essays from 'The Exchange'* will smile, frown, and shake their heads in amazement at this collection of questions and answers.

Each question was really asked of some reference librarian who couldn't answer it and asked for help from other librarians via the 'Exchange' column. Customs, people and places, sayings, and quotations are some of the categories of the queries. Ingenuity and hours of research went into answering many of these puzzles.

Reference librarians will want a copy of the book to supplement their in-house 'hard-to-find' files. Trivia lovers will want to own it for fascinating reading. This would be an excellent bedside table book, gift, or travel read. Highly recommended to those with an ounce of curiosity."

Janice M. Sterner, MLS
Collection Specialist,
Timberland Regional Library

The Haworth Information Press®
An Imprint of The Haworth Press, Inc.
New York • London • Oxford

Puzzles and Essays from "The Exchange"
Tricky Reference Questions

Puzzles and Essays from "The Exchange"
Tricky Reference Questions

Charles R. Anderson, MLS 1935–

The Haworth Information Press®
An Imprint of The Haworth Press, Inc.
New York • London • Oxford

Published by

The Haworth Information Press®, an imprint of The Haworth Press, Inc., 10 Alice Street, Binghamton, NY 13904-1580.

Cover design by Lora Wiggins.

Library of Congress Cataloging-in-Publication Data

Anderson, Charles R., 1935-
    Puzzles and essays from "The exchange" : tricky reference questions / Charles R. Anderson.
        p. cm.
    Compiled from the column that appeared in the journal RQ (later Reference and user services quarterly).
    Includes bibliographical references and index.
    ISBN 0-7890-1761-X (alk. paper)—ISBN 0-7890-1762-8 (pbk.)
    1. Reference services (Libraries). 2. Questions and answers. I. Title.

Z711 .A393 2003
025.5'2—dc21

2002068857

To all the reference librarians who, for thirty-five years, read "The Exchange," searched for, and often found answers to the puzzles in the column, and to Susan, who answered the one really important question.

ABOUT THE AUTHOR

Charles Anderson, MLS, has been a reference librarian for thirty years, serving in libraries from the East Coast to the Midwest to the Northwest. During his library career he has published extensively in library literature and has contributed chapters to books on reference services with emphasis on the effects of computer applications. From 1984 to 1999 he edited the column, "The Exchange" in *RQ* (later *RUSQ*), the official journal of the Reference and User Services Division of the American Library Association. Upon the cessation of "The Exchange" column, Gail Schlachter, then editor of *RUSQ* wrote, "Rarely has one individual facilitated the answers to so many difficult questions, and in such an elegant and entertaining style." He is currently the owner of a freelance indexing business called The-Indexer.com.

CONTENTS

Preface

The contents of this book grew out of a column written for librarians that appeared in the professional journal (*RQ* and later *RUSQ*) of the Reference and User Services Division of the American Library Association. The column was called "The Exchange" except for several early incarnations named "Salmagundi." The purpose of the column, as described in a footnote that appeared at the bottom of the first page of each column, was to serve as a reference librarians' exchange for "Tricky questions, notes on unusual information sources, and general comments concerning reference problems."

For thirty-five years, librarians in the United States and other countries sent "The Exchange" puzzles they could not answer locally. Other readers often furnished answers—sometimes years or even decades later. When an analysis was done in 1985, the track record for questions answered was 47.25 percent. Questions covered all areas of human interest, but 62.2 percent were in the humanities, 3.9 percent in the sciences, 6.4 percent in social science areas, and 27.5 percent had to do with some aspect of library science. Quotations accounted for 41.7 percent of the questions posed, and the next most popular category was word or phrase origins (12.8 percent) ("The Exchange," 1985).

Even when no information was forthcoming, it should be helpful to other librarians to know how extensive a search has been for that elusive answer. For this reason, those questions that were never answered are included in this compilation. The book presents the questions and answers as a reference resource and hopefully as a source of some entertainment as well. Questions are arranged by category, interspersed with short essays (somewhat rearranged, edited, and in some cases updated) that appeared at the beginning of the columns during my editorship. These "sermonettes" or exhortations to the reference librarians of the world present a view of one person's ideal level of library service. They should be taken in just that regard.

Reference librarianship, particularly in a busy library, can be one of the most challenging and yet rewarding occupations possible. Sometimes the question is asked, "What does it take to be a good reference librarian?" Alternatively, when talking to someone not in the field who learns that your chosen career path is that of reference librarian, you may hear a remark to the effect that "you must know an awful lot." Contrary to what some believe, it is not necessary to have a mind that is totally dedicated to trivia. The essential element that makes a good reference librarian is not knowing the answer to every question, but rather having a broad understanding of how to find answers. It is also very helpful to have the kind of mind that can impose order on a wide range of information. Finally, the good reference librarian must possess a healthy sense of curiosity.

It is that healthy sense of curiosity—indeed a curiosity that some might say borders on obsession—that drove some of the readers of "The Exchange." What else would explain those librarians who searched for answers months, years, and even decades after a question appeared in the column? Some reference librarians have even made it a post-retirement career to search out answers to the puzzles that appeared. Many of these puzzles still generate reference interest, even in the days of the Internet.

Recent notices in the library literature have drawn attention to what seems to be a general trend toward decreasing numbers of reference questions in American libraries. The obvious factor contributing to this is the nearly ubiquitous nature of Web access for many library patrons. Although there is obviously no way that unmoderated Web searches can replace the training and talent of reference librarians, the demands of an ever shortening availability of time for users, the continuing explosion of available information, and funding difficulties in many of our libraries have made this development almost inevitable.

Despite this inevitability, somehow the abilities and knowledge that reference librarians have brought to the job over many years need to be retained in the Brave New World of instant access to information. To lose these talents would be to lose something which, while mostly intangible and perhaps not well-recognized over the past century, has brought rewards to those who practice the field and benefits to countless numbers of patrons. I do not know what steps need to be taken to ensure the continued involvement of reference librarians in access to information. I suspect the impetus will have to come from the educational fields. Hopefully, those schools that felt the need to jump on the bandwagon of the information age by renaming themselves "School of Information Science" or something similar will retain enough of a humanistic approach to maintain the "art" of reference librarianship.

As these information science programs focus on preparing graduates in a computer-literate society, hopefully some faculty will retain and communicate the sense of wonder that I still get when I look at the kinds of questions that "The Exchange" was able to answer over the many years that the column appeared. It is also my sincere hope that this small book will contribute to keeping the ideals of reference librarianship alive.

Chapter 1

Strange and Common Customs

Reference librarians enjoy getting certain categories of questions (despite a commitment to giving equal weight to each question) versus other categories that make them unobtrusively grit their teeth. I suspect that questions about peculiar customs that we take for granted would rank high on the favorite list. Certainly these questions about the origins of simple or mysterious customs accounted for a fair percentage of questions that ended up in the files of "The Exchange" over the years. Unlike requests for obscure poems that only the patron's grandmother remembered, or attempts to track mysterious sayings through quotation dictionary after quotation dictionary, the origins of interesting customs can be fascinating. If nothing else, they may improve librarians' chances on *Jeopardy*. For that reason, the Strange and Common Customs category opens the list of questions received from and answered by readers of "The Exchange."

*   *   *

Travelers to Europe with a heightened observational capability sometimes note that some Europeans wear wedding rings on the right hand. Sooner or later, this question turns up in the library.

The choice of ring finger depends on the country. Almost all married people in the United Kingdom and Scandinavia wear a wedding ring on the left hand, as do 50 percent of the wedded people in Germany, the Netherlands, and Switzerland, all of which are predominantly Protestant countries. In Catholic countries such as France, Spain, Italy, Austria, Ireland, and Belgium, it is common to find the right hand used as the ring hand. However, divorcees and widowers frequently change hands.

The English and American custom of using the left hand may have been a novelty of the Reformation. In 1549 Bishop Cranmer, compiling the first *Book of Common Prayer,* changed the practice to the left hand because it was believed there was a vein or nerve in the fourth finger that led directly to the heart (Shepherd, 1950). The European custom of using the right hand could be associated with the right hand being the hand of honor, while the left hand was associated with sinister acts.

How did the custom of giving engagement rings develop?

According to some references, the engagement ring preceded the wedding ring in history. It was an "earnest of future intentions . . . and closely connected with the purchase of women" (Brasch, 1965). Confirming the relationship between the ring and a promise of future action is *Curious Customs* (Tuleja, 1987). The custom may go back to ancient times (McCarthy, 1945), but the actual engagement tradition was born when Pope Innocent III decreed in A.D. 1215 that a waiting period be observed between betrothal and marriage. This led to the tradition of two rings.

During the Middle Ages and Renaissance, jeweled rings became popular. The Venetians are credited with introducing the diamond into the engagement ring picture. The rarity of diamonds until modern times prevented the diamond from being used in the typical engagement ring. For a while, the wedding ring became the main ring, and the use of an engagement ring decreased. However, as the supply of diamonds increased dramatically, the gem became more popular in engagement rings.

One of the ways that Americans stand out as foreigners in other countries is their habit of cutting food with the right hand but then switching the fork from the left hand to the right to eat. Why do they go through this somewhat awkward step?

There are at least two explanations for this custom: (1) to keep the left hand free to grab a rifle at frontier posts; (2) so strangers at the same table can be certain that no one can attack them unexpectedly.

Why do people drive on the left in some countries?

Three of the world's most populous countries use the right side: the United States, Russia, and China. Two others, India and Indonesia (second and fourth in population rank in 2000), use the left side. The rest of the world varies. South Africans, Pakistanis, Sri Lankans, Australians, Thais, Japanese, and the British use the left side. One significant reason for this pattern is that about 90 percent of the human race is right-handed. Until some 200 years ago, this right-handedness favored keeping to the left.

Even in early history, the ancient Greeks, Egyptians, and Romans all observed a left-hand rule for marching their troops. This was because a man could more easily draw his sword to defend against an attack from the right (*Los Angeles Times,* 1984). It was natural for people walking or riding on horseback along roads to edge toward the left when they saw an unknown person approaching from the front. This defensive movement allowed both parties to draw their swords—if that became necessary. This became the general rule, if not a law.

In 1300 A.D. Pope Boniface VII declared that all roads lead to Rome and directed pilgrims to keep to the left side of the road, which some countries have done ever since (Hopper, 1982).

Britain's keep left rule was unwritten common law before the eighteenth century. An ordinance in 1756 ordered drivers going over the London Bridge to keep to the left. In 1772 this rule was extended to Scotland. The penalty for disobeying was 20 shillings. "The General Highways Act of 1773 did not apply the keep-left rule to England. The custom was already established. . . . The keep-left rule did not become law in Britain until 1835, although local regulations existed" (Hamer, 1987).

It was Napoleon who first imposed right-hand driving on Europe (Hopper, 1982). Each conquered country was forced to adopt the custom to show their subordination to the emperor. Lafayette helped spread the custom to the Americas. In the United States, the earliest known law for driving on the right was enacted by the Pennsylvania legislature in 1792 (Hamer, 1987).

Is there any particular meaning to the way that military statuary is posed? For example, does a statue of a horse and rider with two of the horse's feet off the ground mean the rider died in combat?

There is nothing but anecdotal evidence for this belief, and there are many exceptions. General Andrew Jackson's statue in Washington, DC, has forefeet pawing the air, yet Jackson died at home. The New York City statue of General Sherman has two hooves pawing the air, but Sherman died years after the Civil War. Rather than some mythical relationship to the manner of death, the placement of hooves has more to do with architectural and engineering requirements and the skill of the sculptor. When you think about getting a massively heavy statue posed with 98 percent of it off the ground—it is a wonder that any rearing horse statues exist.

Where did the college custom of homecoming originate?

Illinois claims ownership of the origin of this custom. Two members of the class of 1910, Walter Elmer Ekblaw and Clarence Foss Williams, conceived the idea and presented it to university authorities. The first homecoming celebration was held at the October 15, 1910 football game at Illinois Field (*Champaign-Urbana News Gazette*, 1981).

Is there anything more ubiquitous in the academic or business world than the yellow legal pad? Who first thought of making these pads?

According to the American Pad and Paper Company, the pads resulted from the request of a turn-of-the-century judge who "grew tired of penciling horizontal lines on his scratch pads, and needed a vertical line on the left for his marginal notes" (*Los Angeles Times*, 1981).

Of all the different sizes it could be, why is letter-size typing paper 8½ by 11 inches?

The United States government in 1921 changed from a standard of 8 by 10½ inches to the new size as a result of an advisory group called the Permanent Conference on Printing (*Evening Tribune*, 1979). The first attempt at standardizing paper sizes came in the early sixteenth century, according to Hart Phinney of the Institute of Paper and Science Technology in Atlanta. Henry VIII, by royal decree, ordered all paper for printing to be a specific size, since printers all over Europe were using varying sizes (Phinney, 1993).

How did the custom of tying yellow ribbons around trees in memory of captives begin?

Tony Orlando and Dawn recorded a song with the title "Tie a Yellow Ribbon 'Round the Old Oak Tree" in 1973. It was composed by Irwin Levine and L. Russell Brown. The song later was the subject of a plagiarism suit because the story that the song tells appeared earlier in a newspaper article, supposedly a true story (*The Economist*, 1991).

As the story goes, around 1971 a group of young New Yorkers was on a bus to Florida. They saw an elderly passenger sitting silently by himself. He told them he had been in jail for four years. Before he went to prison, he wrote his wife in Georgia, saying he would understand if she didn't want to see him anymore. Before release, he wrote again, telling her he would be on the bus and, if she wanted him to stay, she should tie a yellow handkerchief to the oak tree in town. If he didn't see the handkerchief, he would stay on the bus. When the bus pulled into town, the tree was decorated with hundreds of yellow scarves.

One of the young people told Pete Hamill, a *New York Post* columnist, the story and he wrote a piece about it. It also was summarized in a *Reader's Digest* story. In a slightly different version, described by Curtis Bok, the returning convict wrote to his family asking them to put a white ribbon in the big apple tree near the railroad track if they wanted him back. Afraid to look when he arrived, he had a friend look for him. The friend told him "it's OK because the whole tree is white with ribbons" (Bok, 1959).

Penne Laingen, wife of L. Bruce Laingen, the American Embassy charge d'affaires in Tehran taken as a hostage in 1979, is credited in a newspaper story for having started the yellow ribbon campaign, based on the song (*The New York Times*, 1980).

However, the idea of wearing something in memory of a loved one far away is far older. By 1838, Americans were singing "It's all around my hat that I twine the weeping willow . . . for my true love far, far away" (Spaeth, 1948). *Bawdy Songs and Backroom Ballads* (Brand, 1960) contains a song "Around Her Neck," which describes a young woman wearing a yellow ribbon around her neck for a soldier "far, far away." Brand feels the song "probably goes back to early British vaudeville times when it was known as 'All Round my Hat I Vears a Green Villow'" (Brooks, 1991).

Despite news reports of the practice, Civil War historians were unable to document yellow ribbons being worn by women in the Civil War (Brooks, 1991). John Wayne's movie *She Wore a Yellow Ribbon* took the name from the official color of the U.S. Cavalry (Wormser, 1966).

Never be surprised at what innocuous custom may give rise to a patron's burning curiousity. For example, one library sent in a question asking how long people have been using toothpicks.

A simple toothpick may have been one of the first "tools" of human design. Analysis of grooves on ancient teeth has led to a consensus that these are the marks of heavy toothpick use by human ancestors. The earliest known example of the grooved-teeth phenomenon was found in 1.8 million-year-old fossils of *Homo habilis.* Several other sources provide some additional information (Bennett, 1984; Bremner, 1954; Bahn, 1989; Proskauer, 1946a, 1946b; *Science News,* 1988; Wilford, 1989).

In Denmark, there is a custom of eating duck on November 11. What is the background to this habit?

According to *Festivals of Western Europe* (Spicer, 1958), November 10 is celebrated in Denmark as *Mortensaften* (St. Martin's Eve). There is a legend connected with St. Martin of Tours. St. Martin was hiding in a barn from soldiers intent on taking him to town to be appointed as Bishop. A stupid goose gave away his presence by quacking. The bird lost his neck for his noisiness. *The Book of Days* (Chambers, 1967) simply says that fat geese are in their prime at the time of St. Martin's Festival. Later, duck was substituted for the more expensive goose. Another source notes that Danish people eat goose on November 10 to celebrate Martin Luther's birthday (Wolhrabe and Krusch, 1972; MacHaffied and Nielsen, 1976).

How did the custom of athletic letter awards originate?

Among English universities, the practice of rewarding college athletes with some distinguishing mark was popular. The initial date of this custom is unknown. A *Harper's Weekly* article in 1897 noted that "decades ago" a Committee of Blues (composed of five leading university captains) determined who should have awards, which were known as "blues." Athletes of lesser importance were awarded a "half blue" (Snyder, 1949).

Why do school sweaters worn by high school and college athletes always have two rings on the upper right arm?

Originally, the rings signified how many years the individual had participated in a sport. Now they have become traditional and have no particular meaning (Berkeley Fashions Inc., 1983).

It is easy to find lists of gifts for major anniversaries, but what about all the off years?

The Jewelers of America Association has a pamphlet on the topic, as does *The Hostess Book* (1928). Here are some of the in-between years:

8th—canned goods	33rd—amethyst
9th—iron	34th—opal
21st—brass or nickel	37th—alabaster
22nd—copper	39th—lace
23rd—silver plate	42nd—improved real estate
24th—musical instruments	44th—groceries
26th—original pictures	48th—optical (spectacles, micro-
27th—sculpture	scopes, telescopes)
28th—orchid	49th—luxuries of any kind
29th—new furniture	80th—diamond and pearl
31st—timepieces	85th—diamond and sapphire
32nd—conveyances	90th—diamond and emerald
including automobiles	100th—ten-carat diamond

Some other lists differ in a few respects. For example, pottery may be given as an eighth or ninth anniversary gift (Plumb and Fuller, 1951). Incidentally, the thirteenth is often left out because thirteen was considered unlucky.

Where would the bucolic sport of horseshoe pitching be if someone at some point early in history had not invented the horseshoe? What people first used the horseshoe?

The horseshoe was used by Romans in the first century B.C. A mule losing its shoe is mentioned by the Roman poet Catullus (*Encyclopedia Britannica*, 1976). In an edition of Catullus' poems, a writer comments:

> There is no indication in ancient monuments or writers that the shoes were nailed on. . . . Probably the metal sole . . . was attached to a sort of sock of leather or woven fibre, which was in turn fastened by thongs about the fetlock. Such a shoe might readily be lost in strongly adhesive mud. (Merrill, 1951)

Migratory Eurasian tribes also used horseshoes by the second century B.C. The first nailed iron horseshoe appeared in Europe about the fifth century A.D., introduced by invaders from the East.

Why are the colors pink and blue associated with the birth of girls and boys respectively?

An ancient belief held that evil spirits hovered over the nursery. These spirits were supposedly allergic to some colors, most particularly blue because of its association with the sky. Boys were protected with blue clothes, but girls, being considered much less important, were not given any distinctive color. Pink came later, with some European legends claiming that girls were born inside a pink rose (Brasch, 1965; Feldman, 1986).

Assisting the Tooth Fairy, countless parents have placed innumerable coins under pillows to replace lost baby teeth. The only change over the years has been in the denomination of the coin. I understand Sacagawea dollars are the latest fashionable amount. How did the legend of the Tooth Fairy begin?

There is no single source for this legend. Several book titles by Joseph and Carter contain some information (Carter and Carter, 1987; Carter, n.d.). An English description of the custom can be found in *The Lore and Language of School Children* (Opie and Opie, 1959). According to this source, the practice is a "commercial and apparently modern transaction." Confirming the recent development of this legend, Leo Kanner devoted a chapter in his 1928 book *Folklore of the Teeth* to traditional superstitions regarding the loss of milk teeth but made no mention of anything resembling the Tooth Fairy (Kanner, 1928).

Nevertheless, there may be some connection to St. Apollonia. According to *The Catholic Encyclopedia* (1934), St. Apollonia was a holy virgin who suffered martyrdom in Alexandria during a local uprising against the Christians in approximately 248 A.D. Before being burned to death, all her teeth were broken. "The Roman Church celebrates her memory on February 9, and she is popularly invoked against the toothache because of the torments she had to endure. She is represented in art with pincers in which a tooth is held" (*Catholic Encyclopedia,* 1934).

When did the custom of women shaving their legs become popular?

A lengthy exposition on this appeared in *Femininity* (Brownmiller, 1984).

Leg hair was not a problem to American women before the 1920s because the legs of most women were never on public view. When a change in attitude toward recreation, fashion and female emancipation during the prosperous, post-war Jazz Age made it socially acceptable for women of all ages and classes to expose their limbs, modesty regarding the propriety of showing legs was transformed with astonishing rapidity into a dainty self-consciousness regarding "unsightly" hair. As depilatory advertisements reminded their audiences in the women's magazines, the classic Greek ideal of feminine beauty appeared hairless in sculptural white marble.

Before World War I, women wore voluminous bathing costumes, with long, dark stockings. They took refreshing dips, but did not swim until the 1920s, under the influence of various famous women swimmers. When women did take up swimming, as well as sunbathing, more abbreviated swimming attire became popular. Short dresses for street wear and the national craze for dancing also encouraged a sleekly groomed leg.

Since there is always the risk of breaking a glass, what drives people to clink glasses when drinking a toast?

One theory claims this custom goes back to the ancient practice of pouring wine from one vessel into another to guard against poisoning. The host would offer wine; the guest would pour a little back into the host's glass to make sure the drink was safe. Then each would take a sip at the same time. In time, the reason for the practice was forgotten and people would just clink the glasses together and drink simultaneously.

A second, rather fanciful theory connects this custom with the Jacobites in the 1800s. As the story goes, the Jacobites had to be secretive about their Stuart sympathies because they felt that the reigning king was not the true one. When called upon to drink a toast to the king, they wished to drink to the one "over the water." To show this, they passed their wine glasses over finger bowls before drinking. When the significance of the gesture was discovered, finger bowls were banished. In return, the Jacobites began passing one wineglass over the other, or simply touching the bottom of one glass to the rim of another (Stimpson, 1948). Another theory suggests that the noise produced by clinking, a bell-like ring, was thought to drive evil spirits away.

Why does the Jewish star have six points and the Christian star have five points?

Some information can be found in several sources (Drury, 1992; *Encyclopedia Judaica,* 1971; *Man, Myth, and Magic,* 1982). It appears that the six-pointed Jewish star, called the Magen David (Shield of David, Star of David) in Hebrew, predates written historical records and was used as early as the Bronze Age in areas from Mesopotamia to Britain. In the sources, the emphasis is not upon the number of points, but the result of placing two collateral triangles together so that each has the same center at the face and point in opposite directions. There is no reference to the Star of David in the Bible or in Jewish rabbinical writings.

However, some samples are found in early Jewish synagogues and graves. The symbol has been found more often in non-Jewish contexts. It does not seem to have been distinctly identified with Jewry until after the seventeenth century. It was adopted by the Zionist organization at the First Zionist's Congress in 1897, and is now incorporated in the flag of Israel.

The hexagram also has a place in Western magic and mysticism, embodying the Hermetic axiom "as above, so below." The triangle that points upward symbolizes the masculine, the triangle that points downward the feminine. These triangles are also symbols for fire and water.

The five-point star, a pentagram, has been an important symbol in Western magic, and represents the four elements surmounted by the spirit.

Why are races (horse, auto, sports, etc.) run counterclockwise in the United States and clockwise in England?

During the Revolutionary War, while thoroughbred races were still being run clockwise in the English fashion, an American patriot named William Whitley built a racetrack. To show his patriotism, Whitley decreed that races at his track would be run counterclockwise. However, some races still were run clockwise—for example, Belmont horses raced clockwise until 1921.

There is a historical precedent for the way races are run in the United States. Zenophon believed that horses should be taught to gallop with the near foreleg leading. This is better for a man carrying a spear in his right hand, and on Greek race courses the circuit was always to the left.

> The gallop is not a symetrical gait like the trot. Once the horse is moving, the feet do not in fact alternate, but rather one leg continues to lead with every repetition. If horses do actually prefer to lead with their left . . . it's easier for them to turn towards their left. When leading with the left and turning towards the right, a horse has a tendency to trip. (Caldwell, 1989)

Does someone who saves a life really become responsible for it?

Except for an errant superstition to the effect that saving a drowning man's life was unlucky because it went against the wishes of the gods (Sharper, 1930), quite a few print references to the common belief exist (Albright and Albright, 1980; Steinbeck, n.d.). Most of them seem to be based on the idea that by saving a life, one has altered the natural course of events and thus must take responsibility for this. Albright says, "If you want to heal, what you really are asking is to give life to another person. The only way to give life to another is to give your own life to another, and be prepared to care for him for the rest of his days if necessary." Steinbeck writes, "It was unwritten law in China, so my informant told me, that when one man saved another's life he became responsible for that life to the end of its existence. For, having interfered with a course of events, the savior could not escape his responsibility."

How did the idea of Russian roulette begin?

Lord Byron described an incident of this game in his memoirs as something first played at Cambridge University in 1808 (SCAN, 1978). The description provided the inspiration for "The Fatalist," a short story by the Russian poet and novelist Mikhail Yurievich Lermontov (1814-1841). "The Fatalist" was later issued as part of the novel *A Hero of Our Time* (1840/1958). The gun used in the story, however, was a single-shot pistol, which means the analogy to roulette would be completely wrong.

According to an editor at the *Oxford English Dictionary (OED)*, there is no evidence of a direct connection to Byron or Lermontov.

The first reference in English contexts known to OED are in writings by Graham Greene and G. Surdez, who wrote a short story with the title "Russian Roulette" published in *Collier's* January 30, 1937. Greene does not use the term itself, but he does describe the practice, telling how White Russian officers invented it to overcome their boredom (Burchfield, 1978).

When and where did the custom of taking canaries into mines as early warning devices for carbon monoxide poisoning originate?

This was recommended by Dr. John Scott Haldane in 1895. Haldane was a lecturer in physiology at the University of Oxford. He investigated causes of death among miners in colliery explosions and learned that the cause in many cases was inhalation of carbon monoxide. Haldane suggested that some small, warm-blooded animal such as a mouse or bird could give early warning of a dangerous concentration of the gas (Haldane and Douglas, 1909-1910).

The first actual use of this kind of test was by Dr. W. N. Atkinson, Inspector of Mines for Staffordshire, and Mr. A. M. Henshaw of Talk o' th' Hill Colliery circa 1896. There is no indication whether they used a bird or a mouse. Additional information on using mice and birds to detect carbon monoxide can be found in Burrell (1912) and Weeks (1926).

Why are cigars (rather than something healthy) handed out when a baby is born?

The authority for this is somewhat puzzling. Tyler (n.d.) cites research by the Cigar Institute of America. However, when the Southern California Answering Network (SCAN) contacted the Institute in 1980, they had no record of any such research. Nevertheless, here is a summary of what Tyler wrote:

> The gift of a cigar has always indicated the donor's desire to "share my happiness," and, as far as the Cigar Institute of America has been able to trace it, the custom of giving cigars to celebrate a birth had its origin in just that fashion. In the latter part of the seventeenth century, cigars were quite rare in this country and were treasured, guarded, and in some cases, considered as good as, if not better than, currency of the realm. . . . In those years, the birth of a boy was considered especially important . . . those who could afford to do so gave their friends cigars to note the occasion.

What is the symbolism attached to wearing a flower behind the right ear?

A flower behind the right ear means the wearer is looking for a sweetheart (*Peoples of the Earth,* 1973). In a letter by Rupert Brooke, he describes the custom in Hawaii, saying that a white flower over the left ear means "I have found a sweetheart" (Brooke, 1935). A flower over each ear means "I have one sweetheart and am looking for another." The same symbolism is attached to a red hibiscus worn over the ear (Coats, 1971).

In the old days, outhouses had half-moons carved in the door. What was the purpose and meaning of this symbol?

Early privies were separate for men and women. The woman's privy had a crescent (lunar being feminine) carved in the door while men's privies had a sun (masculine) carving (Sloan, 1963). Later on, "when the country inns became less elegant, the men's outhouse was discontinued because of the proximity of the forests or bushes, and only the outhouse with the crescent remained" (Sloan, 1967). One writer added other purposes: ventilation, conversation, safety, and artistic endeavors. One person claimed that originally a full moon was carved, but people kept getting their heads caught in the door. The hole also allowed those unfortunates who had become trapped inside due to some prankster latching the door from the outside to reach through and "unbutton" the door.

In *The Specialist* (Sale, 1929), the "champion privy builder of Sangamon County" says he can carve stars, diamonds, or crescents. Also popular were twining hearts for newlyweds and bunches of grapes for the newly rich. For another theory, *A Dictionary of Symbols* suggests that "in mediaeval emblems of the western world [a crescent] . . . is a symbolic image of paradise" (Cirlot, 1971). "Perhaps in an emergency on a rainy night when the path is long, the outhouse does take on the feeling of paradise" (Geisey, 1987).

Why is the teenage diversion of everybody switching seats in a car called a Chinese fire drill?

Although the original question posed to "The Exchange" related to the practice of teenagers in a car switching seats, a broader meaning is any "accident scene of great confusion, such as a school bus or cattle truck upset" (Dempsey, 1962). Congressman Robert Wilson used the term to describe the administration of President Kennedy, saying "orders are being issued and countermanded with such frequency that only 'chaos and confusion' remain" (Cray, 1962).

How did the practice of using buttonholes to fasten clothes begin?

It ocurred sometime between the eleventh and fifteenth centuries, but no reader of "The Exchange" ever furnished a closer date (Perica, 1975).

Chapter 2

Reference Commandments for the Twenty-First Century

In 1971 Nathan Josel of the Memphis Public Library provided a set of Ten Reference Commandments. The commandments were adages that most working reference librarians found some truth in as they spent years at the reference desk. As we cope with the challenges of the new millennium, it might be worth looking at how well these commandments stand up—whether some need modification to remain useful in a world of electronic reference. The commandments are in italics, followed by my comments and updated suggestions at the end.

1. The patron is always wrong. This is often explained as meaning that the patron never asks the real question. I suspect it is sometimes used to make library and information science students sit up and smirk. It promotes an Us versus Them mentality that seems, after twenty-five years, just a bit supercilious. Many studies in communication have illustrated how difficult is the task of transferring understanding between two individuals. Entire workshops and numerous articles have been devoted to subjects such as active listening, two-way communication, clarifying and paraphrasing questions, etc. Given all we know now about the problems of understanding a patron's question and responding in a manner that is understandable to the patron, we definitely need a new rule. I propose this simple change: Never assume you understand every question asked.

2. When you know the answer is in a source, it is. That is, after checking all possible sources for an answer, if one stands out as the most likely key to the answer, then you just haven't shaken the pages hard enough for the information to emerge. Unfortunately, as the multitude of new reference books and revised editions of old books has proliferated, the answer that you knew was there may no longer be available. New rule: If the answer should be in a source but you can't find it, it probably was in an older version or in a Web site that no longer exists.

3. Depend on no one's prior research for accuracy or completeness. Modern reference librarians must deal with myriad tasks beyond simply answering questions. New tasks regularly confront reference librarians—dealing with recalcitrant computers, serving as monitors of latchkey children, handling complaints about "pornography" on the Internet, trying to keep current with daily advancements in information technology, etc. Not only can you no longer depend on someone's prior research, it is quite likely that you will be the patron's *only* shot at an answer. My twenty-first-century version of this law: Give every question your best shot; no one else has the time to be as passionate.

4. Coincidence is no coincidence. Josel's example described a patron looking for a biography of Saint Edmund Hall, born 1226. If the librarian finds the same name listed as a college of Oxford University with 1226 as the date of construction, the librarian had best talk to the patron. I don't think the twenty-first century will improve on this one.

5. If it was that hard to find, put it in the query file. Recently I called a local library to ask them to check something that I knew had been in their in-house "hard-to-find" file. I was told that the new head of reference had retired this file because of the Web. The reference librarian on duty said they weren't sure now where to find the hard-to-find file—the height of an ironic answer! This rule is easy to update: If it was that hard to find, put it in the online fugitive facts file.

6. Remember special indexes. These are probably the kind of special indexes that used to be published in pamphlet or small booklet form and almost immediately became lost in the stacks. The most useful alternative is probably the "bookmark" or "favorites" capabilities of Web browsers. These lists, though, can grow to become as unusable as a jumble of unalphabetized index cards. They have to be organized carefully and updated frequently to be useful. My new rule: Create special indexes and bookmarks—and share them online!

7. Use tracings. Do library and information science students still learn about tracings? Will MARC (Machine Readable Cataloging) even be relevant in the coming years? How about: Insist on excellent authority control and automatic cross-references in your online catalog system.

8. Synonyms are the key. Josel advised learning to think in synonyms, or, as he put it, "Learn to adapt the patron's language to those words which sound pleasing to your card catalog." While there still may be control over terms in the library's online catalog, as this catalog becomes simply one node in the Web universe and Web search engines become the standard for retrieving information, a more relevant rule for the twenty-first century might be: Learn to manipulate and use Boolean capabilities for online searching.

9. Keep a list of where you have looked. Unless this list is maintained somewhere in electronic form, it is probably going to disappear among all the other bits and pieces of paper that still are generated at a reference desk. It is not that this is not still valid, but in the light of the present-day real world on busy reference desks, is anyone else going to be as thorough or are you even going to be able to get back to the question? (See commandment 3.)

10. "No" is never an answer. This one should be engraved in titanium for all time. It embodies the primary responsibility of each reference librarian—to meet the commitment each of us takes on when we stand behind a desk labeled "Reference" or "Information." We find the answer, or we find a place where the patron can find the answer, or we suggest another route to try. We never, as one librarian pithily put it, "Negotiate the question out of existence." Perhaps it may help to follow what I term the "lost sheep" philosophy of good reference service. That is, you may answer all the easy questions in the world, but until you find that one last lost question, you have not finished your work.

Over the years I have also formulated two corollaries to these laws:

a. The more certain you are that a question has been answered definitively, the more likely it is that another answer will turn up later.

b. The best answer to a difficult question will either be found several months later when the patron is no longer available, or the previous year, when you weren't even thinking of the question.

Chapter 3

Popular Sayings

A second category with which the busy reference librarian may have a love-hate relationship is the search for the first person to utter some well-known saying or truism. I suspect that in the minds of many patrons there is a touching, albeit naive belief that if an expression is so common, it must be a simple matter to locate its origin in the local library. This attitude is probably at least partially caused by the tendency of governmental agencies to announce (without previously mentioning it to libraries) that such-and-such a publication is "available at your local library." As librarians who wrote to "The Exchange" often demonstrated, this is not always the case. Here is a collection of those popular sayings that did "come home" with answers.

* * *

There is a popular conundrum expressed by the saying, "If a tree falls in a distant forest, and no one is there to hear it, does it make a noise?" Is there any real answer to this question, and if so, who provided it?

If the philosopher George Berkeley had been asked this question, he probably would have said that a tree falling where no one could hear it would not make a noise. In somewhat convoluted prose, he wrote:

> You must distinguish, Philonous, between sound, as it is perceived by us, and as it is in itself; or, (which is the same thing), between sound we immediately perceive, and that which exists without us, and as it is in itself. The former is indeed a particular kind of sensation, but the latter is merely a vibrative or undulatory motion in the air. (Berkeley, 1963)

Another occurrence of this thought appears in a story by Henry Allen in the *The Washington Post Magazine.* Allen wrote:

> . . . get right back to you. Otherwise you'll never know whether I got the message. And if so, would the message exist? I mean, if the tree falls in the woods and there's nobody there to hear it, does it make any noise? I know, this is solipsism. You learned all about it in college. Bishop Berkeley and all that." (Allen, 1987)

We all know "the grass is greener" somewhere else. But who first pointed this out?

An article titled "Folk Sayings in a Pioneer Family of Western Oregon" by Helen Pearce (1946) credits this phrase to "cowboys, miners, and (or) woodsmen." There is a Latin saying to the effect that *Fertillior seges est alienis semper in agris,* or "The crop seems always more productive in our neighbor's field" (Ramage, n.d.).

What Indian tribe originated the saying, "Don't criticize a man until you have walked a mile in his moccasins"?

Since the word "mile" is not part of Indian vocabulary, *moon* is a more likely word in an aboriginal saying than *mile*. One version reads: "Don't judge any man until you have walked two moons in his moccasins." Various authorities say it is traditional among the Indian people, particularly in the northern plains (Demeyer, 1974; Tripp, 1970).

When people refer to "the whole nine yards," what are the yards composed of?

There are probably nine yards' worth of explanations for this phrase. William Safire called this one of the great etymological mysteries of our time (Safire, 1982). Dr. Fred Cassidy, editor of the *Dictionary of American Regional English,* confessed himself to be "thoroughly puzzled."

The most popular explanation goes back to the era of handmade clothes for ladies. Fabric was much rougher than the current machine-made products, and a bolt of material held only nine yards. A very fine dress might require the "whole nine yards." Another idea refers to the contents of a cement mixer truck, which supposedly holds nine cubic yards of cement. A very large job, then, might take the whole nine yards.

There is also a nautical explanation. A square-rigged, three-masted sailing ship carries three yards (the rods supporting the sails) on each mast. The "whole nine yards" would mean the sails were fully set. In each case, the meaning is giving one's full effort to some enterprise. The lexicographer William Safire included some explanations in a column in *The New York Times Magazine* (Safire, 1982).

Who was the fat lady in the saying, "The opera ain't over until the fat lady sings"?

No one knows for certain. Dick Motta popularized this saying during the Washington Bullets' NBA championship drive in 1978, but the idea originated with sports editor Dan Cook. The story goes like this: In 1975 Ralph Carpenter, Texas Tech's information director, remarked to an Austin press box contingent, "The rodeo ain't over till the bull riders ride."

To top this marvelous insight, Dan Cook responded with the opera paraphrase (*The New York Times,* 1980). Motta heard the saying, repeated it several times, and the words became a motto for the team.

There are other versions, though, such as "Church ain't out till the fat lady sings." This was in a 1976 publication that was probably put together before the Texas Tech version. Supposedly the Philadelphia Flyers hockey team always finished their home games with Kate Smith singing "America the Beautiful." However, saying that the game is not over until the fat lady sings implies a state of excess poundage that maligns a fine singer.

What is the origin of the expression "Close, but no cigar"?

This expression is thought to have come from carnival use. As a test of strength, contestants swung a sledgehammer to drive an arrow up a pole and win a cigar. When the arrow failed to reach the top and ring the bell, the barker would say, "Close, but no cigar" (Safire, 1980).

Who originated the saying, "I'd rather be a 'has been' than a 'could have been' "?

Only one attribution was ever produced. This source claimed the phrase was a saying of major league baseball players (Fox, 1992).

As we approached the millennium, the phrase *"fin de siècle"* appeared in some articles. What exactly does it mean?

This French phrase, which translates literally as "end of the century," was closely related to the literary school of decadence, which originated in nineteenth-century France. The actual phrase was associated with the writer Joris-Karl Huysmans (1848-1907). His novel *A Rebours* (1884) has been called the "breviary of the movement" (Becksen and Ganz, 1975). According to Bliss (1966), there was also a novel or play titled *Fin de Siècle* by F. de Jouvenot and H. Micard written in 1888.

What is the meaning of the phrase "going down the tube"?

"In surfing, a tube is a tunnel that forms in the face of a long wave just before the wave breaks. To shoot, or go down the tube, is one object of the sport, although the awkward position it requires led to the derogative, to tube it, to fail." Nonsurfers confused down the tube with down the pipe and down the drain, and "A seaside triumph became a bathroom disaster" (Safire, 1990).

If you escape the tube, then perhaps you should worry about the tunnel. How did the phrase "light at the end of the tunnel" originate?

In the book *Self-Destruction: The Disintegration and Decay of the U.S. Army During the Vietnam Era* (Cincinnatus, 1980), General Eugene-Henri Navarre is credited with being the first person to use the phrase. Cincinnatus obtained his information from an article in *Time* (1953) which attributes the statement to an anonymous acquaintance of the general. Since railroads and tunnels have been around a lot longer, and thinking of the old country and western song that includes the lines, "There's a light at the end of the tunnel; I pray it's not a train!" the sentiment is probably a lot older than the Vietnam era.

What is the story behind the three monkeys who represent "hear no evil, see no evil, speak no evil"?

The three apes are the attendants of Saruta Hito no Mikoto or Koshin, the God of the Roads. They are named Kikazaur, covering his ears, who listens to no evil; Mizaru, with a hand over his eyes, who sees no evil; and Iwazaru, his hand on his mouth, who speaks no evil (Joly, 1967).

Did Confucius say, "One picture is worth a thousand words"?

According to Stevenson (1959), Fred Barnard first used the saying and called it "a Chinese proverb, so that people would take it seriously." Stevenson adds, "It was immediately credited to Confucius."

What was the origin of the expression "Katy, bar the door"?

In 1437, Catherine Douglas, afterward called the "Bar-lass," attempted to prevent the assassins of James I of Scotland from entering the room where the king was hidden by thrusting her arm in the slot which should have held a strong bar. Her fragile arm broke and the king was murdered (*Dictionary of National Biography,* 1921).

Where did the idea that "there's no such thing as a free lunch" come from?

"Free lunch" dates from the 1840s and moved from the West to the East, getting fancier as it approached Eastern bars and hotels. At some point, someone probably said something like, "Pay for that drink first before you get the free lunch!" The famous economist Pareto is supposed to have asked, "Can you tell me a restaurant where I can get a good lunch, free?" He received the reply, "There are no such restaurants." Pareto then said, "There is a general law of economics for you." Alternatively, according to *The Oxford Dictionary of Quotations* (1954), "colloquial axiom in US economics from the 1960s, much associated with Milton Friedman; recorded in the form 'there ain't no such thing as a free lunch' from 1938." Recent information from a Web search confirms an early 1800s date. According to *The Encyclopedia of American Food and Drink,* it was a midday meal offered to saloon customers to entice them in to drink more beer and spirits. One historian contends that the practice began in a hotel in the New Orleans French Quarter circa 1835 and was created for business clientele who could not get home for lunch (Mariani, 1999).

Where did the idea of an "American Dream" begin?

The phrase is at least as old as Alexis de Tocqueville's 1835 writings about America (*Facts on File,* 1987; Morris and Morris, 1988; Safire, 1978). An interesting use of the phrase turned up through a WestLaw search. *McAndrew v. Scranton Republican Pub Co.* referred to the Communist Platform of 1948, which says in part, ". . . we Communists are dedicated to the proposition that the great American dream of life, liberty, and the pursuit of happiness will be realized only under socialism. . . ." It is perhaps indicative of the broadness and lack of specific definition of the phrase that it has migrated from de Tocqueville's *Democracy in America* to a reference in the platform of the Communist party.

What is the origin of the phrase "dustbin of history"?

Trotsky is the usual attribution for this saying. The *Oxford English Dictionary* (1989) quotes "Trotsky relegated his opponents to the dustbin of history." *Socialism in One Country* (Carr, 1958) is the source cited by the *OED*. Trotsky's *History of the Russian Revolution* (Trotsky, 1932) contains this quote: "Go where you belong from now on—into the rubbish-can of history." However, *The Oxford Dictionary of Quotations* (1979) attributes this to Augustine Birrell (1850-1933). The form given in this last source is "the great dust-heap called 'history.'"

Any academic librarian with faculty status is surely familiar with the saying "publish or perish." What college or what administrator first thought of this idea?

While the earliest use found of the exact phrase occurred in 1942 (Wilson, 1942), the link between job security on academic campuses and prolific production of words on paper goes back to a much earlier time. An article in *The Atlantic* (1913) includes these lines: "'Publish what?' said I innocently. 'Pages, no matter what,' said he in a whisper, with a glance to see that no one could overhear."

What is the origin of the expression "to kill the messenger bearing bad news"?

There are four possible sources for this saying:

1. Muhammad Shah (fl. fourteenth century, sultan of the Bahmani kingdom in southern India). In this version, "a ragged messenger arrived one day at the sultan's capital. . . . He was the sole survivor of a massacre. The king was so unhappy with the news, he had the messenger killed."
2. The biblical story of David killing the man who brought the news of Saul's death. However, the messenger was killed because he boasted of killing Saul himself (2 Samuel 1:115, KJV).

3. *Lives of the Noble Grecians and Romans* (Plutarch, 1979) includes this line: "The first messenger that gave notice of Lucullus's coming was so far from pleasing Tigranes that he had his head cut off for his pains."
4. There is an engraving by J. J. A. Lecomte-du-Nuoy titled, *The Bearers of Evil Tidings Slain.* According to the librarian who wrote about this engraving, it was inspired by Théophile Gautier's "Mummy" (Berquam, 1990).

Even though there is no monolithic Bell Telephone Company anymore, the nickname "Ma Bell" persists in the minds of many. How did this nickname originate?

I wish "The Exchange" had been able to provide a definitive answer to this one. However, even the Public Relations Department of AT&T was not able to pin down an answer (Gunn, 1986). The PR office believes it was created by someone outside the company, because one employee recalled hearing a newspaper editor use the phrase in a speech about the telephone company. Stuart Flexner, in *Listening to America,* claims Ma Bell became a popular name in 1947 during a strike against Bell Telephone (Flexner, 1982).

However, a story in *Long Lines Magazine* in 1967 said that Sydney Hogerton, *Long Lines* general manager until 1941, recalled hearing the term when he first came to work in 1900.

Another possible origin is that the nickname came from an acquaintance of Alexander Graham Bell. While at Boston University he met a lawyer with a daughter named Mabel. Scarlet fever caused Mabel to go deaf. The daughter became Bell's pupil and later they married. Bell, who spoke French, referred to his wife as "Ma Belle" (my beautiful woman) (Larsen, 1984). Finally, various theories exist to the effect that the nickname came from AT&T's parental steadiness in continuing to pay its famous $9 dividend during the depths of the depression; that Ma Bell reflects the character of the old-time chief operator who always took care of her girls; or that Ma Bell, like Mom, always knew best and offered customers a phone of any color they wanted so long as it was black.

One of the high points of legislative equivocation came when a Congressman was queried about his feelings regarding whiskey. What exactly did he say?

While no specific elected representative has ever, to my knowledge, taken credit for the story, at least one—Congressman D. R. (Billy) Matthews of Florida—repeated the story on a record album (Cameo).

> A Mississippi state senator, being asked how he felt about whiskey, replied: "If, when you say whiskey, you mean the devil's brew, the poison scourge, the bloody monster that defiles innocence . . . then certainly, I am against it with all of my power."
>
> "But if, when you say whiskey, you mean the oil of conversation, the philosophic wine, the stuff that is consumed when good fellows get together, that puts a song in their hearts and laughter on their lips . . . then certainly I am in favor of it."
>
> "This is my stand. I will not retreat from it; I will not compromise." (Gross, 1983)

Whoever the originator of the previous saying was, there is probably no doubt that he or she was capable of both vertical and lateral thinking. The exact meaning of these types of thinking was the subject of another query to "The Exchange."
Vertical thinking is the traditional way, where "one moves forward by sequential steps, each of which must be justified. . . . In lateral thinking one may deliberately seek out irrelevant information; in vertical thinking one selects only what is relevant" (De Bono, 1970). "In problem-solving, vertical thinking elaborates methods for overcoming obstacles in the chosen line of approach, while lateral thinking tries to bypass them by switching to a radically different approach" (Bullock and Stallybrass, 1977).

"The Exchange" covered questions from all walks of life—and death. From the morbid side came a question about the origin of the term "Grim Reaper."
The *OED* suggests that the first use in English was in Longfellow's *The Reaper and the Flowers* (1839). However, the image of death with a scythe "is found on fifteenth-century woodcuts, in religious poetry, and on seventeenth-century tombstones." Andrew Marvell's poem, "Damon the Mower," ends with the line, "For, Death, thou art a Mower too" (Neaman and Silver, 1983).

If the Grim Reaper is after you, maybe the best thing to do is to just say, "Goodbye cruel world." Who originated this depressing sentiment?

Although "Goodbye Cruel World" is the title of a song made popular by James Darren in 1961, a very similar phrase was used by Ralph Waldo Emerson in a poem titled "Goodbye." It begins with the words, "Goodbye proud world."

On a more upbeat note, someone asked "The Exchange," "Who thought up the old saw about today being the first day of the rest of your life?"

Common wisdom has it that this line was used in a speech given by Charles Dederich, the founder of Synanon, around 1969. One "Exchange" contributor claimed that Thomas Wolfe used these words but was not able to cite a specific source. Supposedly, the line also appears in Abbie Hoffman's *Revolution for the Hell of It* (1968). Another author sometimes credited with this saying is Jean Paul Sartre (Walker and Walker, 1973).

What is the exact wording of the saying, "All the world's a bit odd, except for thee and me," and who first noticed this?

There are different forms of this expression in various quotation dictionaries. One source ascribes it to a Quaker speaking to his wife, saying, "All the world is queer except me and thee, and sometimes I think thee is a little bit queer" (Bartlett, 1980). Another version is "All the world is queer save thee and me, and even thee art a little queer" (Evans, 1969; *Macmillan Dictionary of Quotations*, 1989).

A third way of putting this sentiment is, "The only really normal people are the ones you don't know very well." In Emerson's (1968) journals, the following appears: "Sanity is very rare; every man almost, and every woman, has a dash of madness, and the combinations of society continually detect it."

What is the source of the Serenity Prayer? ("O God, give us serenity to accept what cannot be changed, courage to change what should be changed, and the wisdom to distinguish the one from the other.")

An early version in German can be found on the dedicatory page of Christoph Dunker's (1973) *Ausblick von der Weibertreu: Kirchen im*

Bezirk Weinsburg. The German version reads: *"Gib mir Gelassenheit, Dinge hinzunehmen, die ich nicht ändern kann, Den Mut, dinge zu ändern kann, und die Weisheit, das eine vom ändern zu unterscheiden."*

This version is attributed to Johann Christoph Oetinger, Dean in Weinsberg from 1762 to 1769. However, a patron who attended an Alcoholics Anonymous lecture in South Dakota took notes that identified the author as Fredrich Olenger (1702-1780). Librarians at the Union Theological Seminary, where Reinhold Niebuhr was a faculty member for many years, believe Niebuhr was the originator of the English prayer. He was responsible for including this in *A Book of Prayers and Services for the Armed Forces* (Union Theological Seminary, 1978). Niebuhr himself claimed that he didn't consciously adapt this from other sources. In *The AA Grapevine* (1950), he wrote, "of course it may have been spooking around for years, even centuries, but I don't think so. I honestly believe that I wrote it myself." The Anglican publishing house Mobray of London has long identified this prayer as a general or common prayer of fourteenth-century England (*Notes and Queries, 1970*). Another person who may have had some part in its origin is Admiral Thomas C. Hart (1877-1971) (Watson, 1951).

The version preferred by Niebuhr is:

God, give us grace to accept with serenity
The things that cannot be changed.
Courage to change the things which should be changed,
and the wisdom to distinguish the one from the other.

Ursula L. Niebuhr, his widow, believed he may have used the prayer as early as 1934, but it was not in circulation until 1941 or 1942 (Niebuhr, 1978).

According to popular wisdom, if you give a man a fish he will eat for a day, but if you teach him to fish he will eat all his life. Although when you think about it the man probably would get rather sick of finny fare, where did this saying originate?

Some quotation dictionaries claim this is a Chinese proverb from the *Kuantzu*, a philosophical work of ancient China. The common version is: "Give a man a fish and you feed him for a day. Teach a man to fish, and you feed him for a lifetime" (Tripp, 1970).

What is the origin of the saying, "Give us a boy at a tender age and he'll be ours for life"?

There is a saying, supposedly a Jesuit maxim, that reads, "Give me a child for the first seven years, and you may do what you like with him afterwards" (Lean, 1903). Muriel Spark wrote, in *The Prime of Miss Jean Brodie,* "Give me a girl at an impressionable age, and she is mine for life" (Bartlett, 1980).

How did the idea that nice things come in small packages get started?

We can trace this back at least as far as thirteenth-century France, which had this proverb, *"menue[s] parceles ensemble sunt beles."* This translates as "small packages considered together are beautiful" (Simpson, 1982). A Scottish proverb has "good gear goes in sma' book" (translated as "good things are wrapped up in small parcels" (Benham, 1907).

Was it a man or woman who first noted that "behind every great man stands a woman"?

There are a number of variations of this saying, including "The road to success is filled with women pushing their husbands along" (Stevenson, 1967). Elbert Hubbard, wrote (in his short biography of James Oliver), "The man who succeeds is the one who is helped by a good woman" (Hubbard, 1913). Writing about British Prime Minister MacMillan, Godfrey Winn (1963) concluded, "No man succeeds without a good woman behind him. Wife or mother, if it is both, he is twice blessed indeed." Hubert Humphrey (1964) said, "Behind every successful man stands a surprised mother-in-law." Last but not least, John Lennon (quoted in 1979) said, "As usual, there's a great woman behind every idiot" (Rees, 1996).

Sometimes it may be necessary for that woman to give the great man a push. Perhaps this is the reason for the saying, "when push comes to shove." Where did this originate?

Supposedly Senator Edward Kennedy used this saying in a campaign speech, and someone furnished two more lines, reading, "It's time to back away / and let cool heads come into play." The *Dictionary of the Underworld* (Partridge, 1978) says it means "if worse comes to worse, c. p. especially among prostitutes; since about 1920."

"Laundry list" is such a common phrase that you might not expect any patron to wonder about its origin. However, the phrase did end up with "The Exchange."

No specific date for a first use turned up, although the term was in *The Barnhart Dictionary of New English Since 1963* (Barnhart et al., 1973), which gives a clue as to the time of origin. Examples in this source are taken from the political arena. The connection given is to a list of items sent off to a commercial laundry. Safire (1972) defines laundry list as "A long, soporific list of items in a speech, or a series of patronage requests by a political supporter after a successful campaign."

Where did the famous "Desiderata," sometimes cited as "Found in Old St. Paul's Church, Baltimore, dated 1692" actually originate?

The piece was written by Max Ehrmann in 1922 and included in a booklet compiled by the Rector of St. Paul's, one Rev. Frederick War Kales, in 1956. A bibliography for Max Ehrmann lists the poem, with publication in 1927. A parody, titled "Deteriorata," was included on a 45 rpm record with the National Lampoon label, from Blue Thumb LP Radio (Banana Records, 1972). The latter version begins:

> Go placidly amid the noise and waste and remember what comfort there may be in owning a piece thereof. Avoid quiet and passive persons unless you are in need of sleep. Rotate your tires. Speak glowingly of those greater than yourself and heed well their advice even though they be turkeys.

There are 250 more words, ending with "Therefore make peace with your God whatever you conceive Him to be: Bearded Thunderer or Cosmic Muffin. With all its hopes, dreams, promise and urban renewal, the world continues to deteriorate. Give up" (Lynch, 1973).

An expression that could describe reference librarians after a full day on a busy reference desk is that they are on "cloud nine." Where did this description originate?

The phrase "up on cloud nine" was used in the early 1950s in a radio series titled *Johnny Dollar,* which had a recurring scene. When the hero was knocked unconscious, he was transported briefly to "cloud nine." There he could go right on talking. A somewhat more scientific explanation came from a P. T. Lynch of the U.S. Weather Bureau. The following is extracted from Lynch's comments (Morris and Morris, 1962):

> Weather observations are transmitted throughout the world by radio and teletype using a numerical coding system. This system consists of six basic groups of numbers with provision for supplementary groups. Clouds are divided into three main classes and each in turn is divided into nine different types. There are three clouds of type No. Nine. The "low nine" cloud is the cumulo-nimbus or thunderstorm cloud. This is the most majestic cloud with the greatest vertical development. This may be the cloud that is meant by the expression up on cloud nine.

Who was the first butler to be accused of murder, as in "the butler did it"?

Supposedly this comes from a book by Mary Roberts Rinehart (1876-1958). Unfortunately, the source did not identify the title of the book (*Pittsburgh Post-Gazette*, 1993).

A once-popular grandmotherly saying, according to some readers, was "Don't act like Miss Lizzie Tish." Who was Lizzie Tish?

The "Tish" probably came from Mary Roberts Rinehart's *Adventures of Letitia Carberry,* which had a character named Tish, an intrepid old maid. She had two companions in adventure, Lizzie and Aggie. Letitia was called Tish and somehow the first name migrated to a last name (Benét, 1948). This does seem a bit of a leap, but no other reader ever produced any other suggestion.

San Francisco is a beautiful town with a wonderful climate most of the year. But some wag once observed, "The coldest winter I ever spent was one summer in San Francisco." Who said this?

This has been attributed to Arthur Conan Doyle, Robert Louis Stevenson, and H. L. Mencken. In a *New York Times* story, the quote was attributed to Mark Twain (Caen, 1975). However, there is some doubt about this, because in Twain's *Roughing It* there is nothing but praise for San Francisco weather. A more specific source never turned up.

Did Mark Twain say, "When I was fourteen, I thought my old man was an awful fool, but by the time I was twenty-one, I was amazed at how much he had learned in seven years?"

This is probably another case of hopeful attribution. It has never been definitively established as a Twain quote. The lines appeared in the *Reader's Digest* (September 1937) without a source or date. They were also attributed to Twain in *The American Treasury* (Fadiman, 1955). According to the experts at the Mark Twain Collection, Rare Books Department, University of California at Berkeley, it is somewhat improbable that Twain would have said this, since his own father died when he was twelve years old.

Chapter 4

The Ambiguous Library

For centuries, the word "library" meant a collection of written materials surrounded by walls. In the 1980s those walls began to fall. From the great Alexandrian library in the early years of the first millennium through the medieval libraries and into the twentieth century, libraries essentially warehoused written material. Beginning with military defense networks and expanding to research centers, and finally to the worldwide Internet and Web, the trend has been to expand the outer limits of the library building—to break down the walls and make information not only in libraries but also in other types of institutions, even individually published documents, available on a worldwide electronic basis.

Many libraries are now better defined not by physical space, but rather by the limits of electronic access. Instead of printed collections, the contents of libraries are beginning to consist of an existential collection of bits in cyberspace. This new cyberspace dimension involves access to quantities of information far beyond anyone's previous concept of a library.

As the amount of information has increased, the ability to store larger and larger quantities of data has expanded exponentially. We are nearing the point where the amount of data stored in digital form, hence theoretically available to anyone, anywhere, with the proper equipment, is reaching an almost incomprehensible size. The only real way to comprehend such large numbers is to expand the mind gradually from an understandable point.

Beginning with the smallest meaningful element of data in a computer, a bit, one can start to conceptualize these quantities through the following approximation:

- 10 bytes = a single word.
- 10 kilobytes = an encyclopedia page.

- 10 megabytes = Shakespeare's complete works.
- 10 gigabytes = 325 feet of books.
- 10 terabytes = the Library of Congress printed collection.
- 10 petabytes = the world's academic research libraries.
- 500 petabytes = all online data by the year 2000 (500,000,000,000,000,000 bytes).

A 500 petabyte library implies not just a quantitative change in how we will deal with library service—it means a fundamental change in librarianship.

In this new concept of a library, the physical limitations of a structure are irrelevant. Thinking about how we will serve the public in the new library is not an easy task. Nor will the coming changes be an easy transition for current librarians. We are accustomed to thinking in terms of tangible objects—a page, a tape, a video. We think in terms of specific locations—a room, a floor, an aisle, a stack. Most of all, we think of Certainty. A reference book that was classified 016.7 yesterday will be classified 016.7 tomorrow, next week, next decade (barring occasional revisions of Dewey!). A reference librarian will always find a certain answer by going to a certain spot in the collection.

However, the operative word for cyberspace libraries is not Certainty. It is Ambiguity—a difficult concept for most people and most certainly a difficult mode of operation for reference librarians.

The new library collections are not tangible. They are existential, existing only as bits—states of electrical charges—on or off. The collections are constantly changing, mutating, growing, adapting to the environment. In short, these collections have a lot in common with living organisms. Like living organisms, predictability of behavior is uncertain. The path to particular pieces of information may change constantly (Anderson, 2001).

At a joint ALCTS/RUSA institute ("Virtually Yours—Models for Managing Electronic Resources and Services"), one of the speakers noted that the average life span of a Web page was seventy-five days. Currently, a significant amount of labor is spent in libraries bookmarking sites, adding Web page links to library pages, adding URLs to MARC records, or otherwise trying to keep track of useful Web sites for reference. Despite these valiant efforts, one constantly finds dead URLs on even some of the outstanding library Web sites that staff are desperately trying to keep current. Keeping track of sites, even with automated URL checkers, has become a very staff-intensive operation if a library attempts to keep its pages up-to-date.

Supposedly, we are trying to move from the idea of buying many reference books "just in case someone needs them" to accessing information "just in time." However, I am beginning to wonder if we are headed to a future where we will be spending an inordinate amount of time trying to keep up with live Web pages that we never actually get to use. Even when we do find useful sites, how likely is it that URL will be active six months later?

As a small object lesson in bits versus picas, I offer the following example. Recently I worked on a question about "the Lady of the Lake," a mysterious event in a small Washington town. According to the patron, the story was featured on the TV program *Unsolved Mysteries*. Being a proactive Web searcher who sometimes tends to rely on hope and intuition more than the multitudinous Web search engines, my first thought was to see if the TV program had a Web site. I took a guess and entered <www.unsolved.com> as a URL. Lo and behold, the site was there, but there was no mention of this particular episode. I then resorted to an old-fashioned reference source—a directory of newsletters (which I still refer to as Ayer's even though Gale took it over years ago) and the telephone. A one-minute call to the local newspaper in the town found someone who knew the story well (which actually took place ten-plus years ago), and the person was kind enough to fax several stories to me. I thought briefly about bookmarking the Web site and decided that it would be much more helpful simply to add a copy of the newspaper information to our "hard-to-find" file.

The lesson to me here is that we cannot afford to become overreliant on electronic information, particularly given its relative impermanence, and neglect the need for retaining the more permanent hard copy. In other words, the archival role of libraries in an electronic age is fast becoming a vital need.

How prepared is the current generation of reference librarians to serve as mediators between the information in petabyte-sized libraries and the public? What is your institution doing to help you make this transition? How many reference librarians really want to make the needed changes to deal with the future? Of all the tricky questions in "The Exchange" over the years, I find this these among the most difficult to answer.

As I watch the role and function of reference librarians changing, it seems that many of us are becoming stewards of "black" (more frequently buff, cream, or off-white) boxes. I see reference librarians spending less and less time working from a reference desk. Instead, staff are spending increasing amounts of time in a one-on-one teaching role, helping patrons become efficient end-user searchers of the electronic libraries of the world.

As I ponder the long-term future of our profession, I have to wonder how long this teaching role will be necessary. There is a large bulge in the population of library users that still has limited or no computer use experience. However, in another generation, this almost certainly will not be the case. As today's children, who often exceed in their understanding and use of online skills than even our own staff, become adults, what will the reference librarian's role be then? Heretical as it may seem coming from someone who earned an MLS in 1969, I even wonder if the traditional Master's in Library Science degree is the right preparation for the kind of staff we will need in the coming years.

I read essays that foresee librarians being experts in organizing and sifting electronic information sources for the best answers to questions. The authors usually conclude there will be even more important roles for librarians in the twenty-first century. I have seen extended discussions on listservs such as Web4Lib about indexing the Web. I have every respect for the background, knowledge, and professional thought and time that many of these writers put into the topic. However, I have this nagging feeling that they don't really get it. They are talking about indexing and organizing an entity whose complexity is approaching, if not close to exceeding, the complexity of the human brain. We still do not have a clear understanding of the functioning of the brain. Nor do we use more than a small percentage of the brain's theoretical capabilities. Is it realistic to think that we can index a collection of electronic bits of data that changes and grows every second, with an interconnectivity that is becoming infinite?

I sense, moreover, that our users—at least in a public library—are more and more interested in *immediacy*. Information, if it is to be useful, has an increasingly short demand cycle. As the interaction speed with electronic information increases, user expectations for a useful time frame for receiving information are compressed. Perhaps there is some connection with the "television generation" and instant news. "I need this information now—not next week or even tomorrow!" Whether the question is business, homework, consumer related, or even just of a philosophical nature, the reference world is moving into the fast-food age of information.

Chapter 5

Quotations: Spurious and Real

Now we come to one of the most challenging and frustrating types of questions that appear at a reference desk. Searching for elusive quotations is always complicated by the realization that in many cases, in the words of an excellent book, *They Never Said It* (Boller and George, 1989). Another highly readable reference book on the subject of spurious quotes is *Nice Guys Finish Seventh* (Keyes, 1992). Finally, for the serious searcher of lost quotations, there is the definitive *The Quote Sleuth; A Manual for the Tracer of Lost Quotations* (Shipps, 1990).

*　　*　　*

Someone once described success as living well, laughing often, and loving much. Exactly how does this quotation go and who said it?

Although this quotation is often attributed to Ralph Waldo Emerson, it was actually penned by Bessie A. Stanley (1911). The full lines read:

> He has achieved success, who has lived well, laughed often, and loved much; who has gained the respect of intelligent men and the love of little children; who has filled his niche and accomplished his task, whether by an improved poppy, a perfect poem, or a rescued soul; who has never lacked appreciation of earth's beauty, or failed to express it; who has always looked for the best in others and given the best he had; whose life was an inspiration and whose memory a benediction.

Shipps (1976) notes that Bessie (Mrs. Arthur J.) Stanley received an award of $250 in November 1905 from the George Livingston Richards Company. A list of prizewinners, with Mrs. Stanley's name leading all the rest, was printed in the company's magazine, *Modern Women,* for December 1905. The "success definition" still appears in print in various sources. The exact text as it has appeared over the years varies slightly. However, Mrs. Stanley's son, Judge Arthur J. Stanley, says the version given in the eleventh edition of *Bartlett's Familiar Quotations* is the correct one.

On the same theme as the "success definition", there is this quotation: "To be nobody but yourself in a world which is doing its best night and day to make you just like everybody else, means to fight the greatest battle there is to fight and never stop fighting." Who said this?

This was some advice given by e. e. cummings in "A Poet's Advice to Students" (cummings, 1965).

Another question of the inspirational quotation type was a request for the source of "Think like a man of action; act like a man of thought."

Henri Bergson produced this homily. The original version read: *"Je dirais qu'il faut aigr en homme de pensée et penser en homme d'action."* This line is the last sentence of "Message au Congrè Descartes," sent to Emile Bréhier, president of the organization committee, when Bergson, then honorary president of the International Congress of Philosophy, was prevented from joining the delegates (Mossé-Bastide, 1957; *Nouvelle littéraires,* 1937).

Continuing in this vein of inspirational thoughts, who said, "the sands of time are littered with the bones of those who stopped to rest, and resting died"?

Governor Adlai Stevenson, in a campaign speech referring to the Korean War, said, "On the plains of hesitation bleach the bones of countless millions who, at the dawn of victory, sat down to wait—and waiting died." The quotation was attributed to a "William Lawrence." N. W. Ayer and Son, Inc., said "William Lawrence" was the pen name of ad writer George C. Cecil of Philadelphia. Cecil, who became a vice president of the company, wrote the lines in 1922 in an ad to point out what might happen to the reader who failed to take advantage of a correspondence school mail-order education (*San Francisco Examiner,* 1952).

Who said there are three kinds of people: "Those who make things happen; those who watch what goes on; and those who don't know what happened?"

Nicholas Murray Butler, once president of Columbia University, said this (Usher, 1967).

One more uplifting exhortation came to "The Exchange" in 1971. A patron wanted the origin of "Before the gates of Excellence the high gods have placed sweat; long is the road thereto and steep and rough at first."

Very similar lines are found in Hesiod (1959). Several translations conclude with "But when one has reached the top, easy it is thereafter despite the hardness."

Who said, "If I had my life to live over, I would try to make more mistakes next time. I would relax. . . . Ride on more merry-go-rounds . . . pick more daisies"?

Dr. Frank Dickey, an educator, uttered these thoughtful words. The quotation can be found in *Golden Harvest* (Hays, 1979).

If all of the previous self-directed, inspirational thought makes you faint, then perhaps the source of the quotation, "I feel faint; give me a ham sandwich" will be of interest.

This last bit of inspiration is from *Alice's Adventures in Wonderland and Through the Looking Glass* (Carroll, 1970).

Who said, "You ought to get out of those wet clothes and into a dry martini"?

Usually attributed to Robert Benchley, it originated with either actor Charles Butterworth or Mae West (*Los Angeles Times,* 1985).

Who said, "No man who hates dogs and children can be all bad"?

Leo Rosten is often credited with the remark about W. C. Fields; however, this was first said by Byron Darnton of *The New York Times* about an otherwise obscure man named Gastonbury (*Los Angeles Times Calendar,* 1986).

What is the original source of this item that appeared in the "Points to Ponder" column of *Reader's Digest* (1979): "Oh, the

comfort, the inexpressible comfort, of feeling safe with a person; having neither to weigh thoughts nor measure words."

This was originally published in *A Life for a Life* (Craik, 1903). In context, the quotation reads:

> Oh, the comfort—the inexpressible comfort, of feeling *safe* with a person—having neither to weigh thoughts nor measure words, but pouring them right out, just as they are, chaff and grain together; certain that a faithful hand will take and sift them, keep what is worth keeping, and then with the breath of kindness blow the rest away.

Out of context, the following quote seems quite puzzling: "Every man is somewhat dull and somewhat mad; he keeps a fool at court and holds a lunatic in leash." However, when the original source was located, and the correct phrasing found, it made a bit more sense.

This is from one of George Santayana's essays, "Reason and Common Sense" (Darrah, 1939; Santayana, 1905). The phrases are broken up in the relevant text: "Every animal is somewhat dull and somewhat mad. . . . The intelligent man known to history flourishes within a dullard and holds a lunatic in leash. . . . Thus the best human intelligence is still decidedly barbarous; it fights in heavy armor and keeps a fool at court."

Gandhi is supposed to have said something about "need versus greed." What is the full quotation?

The source, as best as can be determined, appears to have been a book by Gandhi's long-time secretary and official biographer titled *Towards New Horizons* (Pyarelal, 1959). It reads, "Earth provides enough to satisfy every man's need but not for every man's greed." The quote is repeated in *Small Is Beautiful* (Schumacher, 1999).

What is the last line of this quotation? "All things are determined, the beginning and the end. We dance to an immutable tune."

One source attributes these lines to Einstein (Campbell and Campbell, 1936). The context reads, "I claim credit for nothing. Everything is determined, the beginning as well as the end, by forces over which we have no control. We all dance to a mysterious tune, intoned in the distance by an invisible player."

Who thought of the phrase "China is a sleeping dragon"?

Supposedly it was Napoleon, who, along with others such as Emerson, is a favorite recipient of quotation attributions. Exhaustive research has never located this aphorism in Napoleon's works. However, several books on China do include this version: "China? There lies a sleeping giant. Let him sleep, for when he wakes he will move the world" (Snow, 1939; Payne, 1950). After Napoleon's death, a flood of pro-Napoleon writings appeared, crediting him with many sayings that cannot be verified.

The closest identified remark on the subject was reported by Barry O'Meara (1822), Napoleon's personal physician on St. Helena. His memoir included these lines: "If I were an Englishman, I should esteem the man who advised a war with China to be the greatest living enemy of my country. You would be beaten in the end, and perhaps a revolution in India would follow."

Another political quotation request was for the origin of "The Mediterranean is the ocean of the past, the Atlantic is the ocean of the present, and the Pacific is the ocean of the future."

Although there is no solid evidence, there is a good case to be made for this being said by John Milton Hay (1838-1905). Hay was involved with negotiations on the Panama Canal, the "Open Door" policy with China, the Spanish-American War, and the acquisition of the Philippines (*Dictionary of American Biography,* 1928-1937). Given these interests, it seems quite reasonable that Hay could have formulated the prescient quotation.

Did Lenin actually say, "The United States . . . will fall into our hands like a ripe fruit"?

President Reagan often quoted this, attributing it to Lenin, but no one has ever found it in any of Lenin's writings or speeches (Herman, 1986).

What is the source of "History is a bag of tricks played upon dead men"?

Durant's (1926) *The Story of Philosophy* attributes this to one of Voltaire's letters to a Mme. du Chatelet. The lines actually read "History is after all nothing but a pack of tricks which we play upon the dead."

Although Emerson is one of those to whom errant quotations seem to stick, he actually did say something about how a man is known by the books he reads.

The full quotation is "A man is known by the books he reads, by the company he keeps, by the praise he gives" (Taylor and Whiting, 1958). According to the original source cited by Taylor *(The Journals of Ralph Waldo Emerson)*, the lines were written June 30, 1880. The sentiment has been expressed by other writers. *Christian Perfection* (Law, 1986) includes this phrase: "We say that a man is known by the friends he keeps, but he is better known by his books" and the same idea is attributed to Euripedes: "Every man is like the company he is wont to keep" (Hoyt's, 1940).

Who felt that, "What I am to be, and now becoming."

There is a very close approximation found on numerous Web sites attributed to both Theodore Roosevelt and Benjamin Franklin that reads, "What I am to be, I am now becoming."

There is a song that includes the lines, "a ragamuffin husband and a rantipoling wife." What is the name of the song?

This is from a little ditty called "Oh Cruel," which can be found in *The Universal Songster, or Museum of Mirth* (1828). The requested lines occur about midway through the song and read:

> Oh! Cruel vas the splinter that broke my poor love's leg,
> Now he's obliged to fiddle for't, and I'm obliged to beg;
> A vagabonding vagrant, and a rantipoling wife,
> We fiddles, and we limps it, through the ups and downs of life.

Who said, "There are few earthly things more beautiful than a University"?

John Masefield said this in an address delivered when he was granted an honorary degree by the University of Sheffield in June 1946. Here is an extract from his words *(The New York Times Book Review, 1971)*:

There are a few earthly things more beautiful than a University
. . . . It is a place where those who hate ignorance may strive to
know, where those who perceive truth may strive to make others
see; where seekers and learners alike, banded together in a
search for knowledge, will honor thought in all its finer ways,
will welcome thinkers in distress or in exile.

**On the other hand, someone once said, "Academic politics are so
bitter (vicious) because the stakes are so small (little)." Who was
this?**

There are several versions of this, one of which is attributed to
Henry Kissinger (Frisch, 1990). Attorney General Edward Levi, former president of the University of Chicago, is supposed to have said,
"Academic politics is the lowest form of politics: trivial, bitter, inse-
cure" (Finnegan, 1991).

**Thomas Jefferson is another who, like Emerson, is frequently
listed as the source of anonymous quotations. One such line was,
"Let us hear no more of trust in men."**

This is a somewhat garbled version of something Thomas Jefferson said: "In questions of power, then, let no more be heard of confi-
dence in men, but bind him down from mischief by the chains of the
Constitution" (*Jeffersonian Cyclopedia*, 1900).

**Another quotation often attributed to Jefferson is, "If the Ameri-
can people ever allow private banks to control the issue of their
currency, first by inflation and then by deflation, the banks and
the corporations that will grow up around them will deprive the
people of all property until their children wake up homeless on
the continent their fathers conquered."**

This particular quotation is probably spurious. According to the
Oxford English Dictionary, the earliest use of "deflation" is 1920.

**"The Exchange" was asked to identify the origin of another
quote from early U.S. history, "Democracy contains within itself
the seeds of its own destruction."**

One writer claimed this could be attributed to Alexis de Tocqueville (Tindall, 1978). However, the sentiment was expressed in various ways by a number of writers. For example, John Adams said,
"Remember, democracy never lasts long. It soon wastes, exhausts,

and murders itself. There never was a democracy yet that did not commit suicide" (Platt, 1993). Attributed to an English writer (Alexander Fraser Tytler, Lord Woodhouselee), but unverified, is this quote:

> [Democracy] can only exist until the voters discover that they can vote themselves largesse from the public treasury. From that moment on, the majority always votes for the candidates promising the most benefits from the public treasury, with the result that a democracy always collapses over loose fiscal policy, always followed by a dictatorship. (Platt, 1993)

Who originated the belief that "Europe begins at the Pyrenees"?

Although Alexandre Dumas was suggested, no proof was ever found (Holcomb, 1970).

What is the source of the following rather pessimistic view of capitalism? "When the rich assemble to concern themselves with the business of the poor, it is called charity. When the poor assemble to concern themselves with the business of the rich, it is called anarchy."

These lines are from the *The Scourge of Christ* (Richard, 1929).

What exactly did Abraham Lincoln say about angels swearing he was right?

Lincoln said, "I do the very best I know how—the very best I can; and I mean to keep doing so until the end. If the end brings me out all right, then what is said against me won't amount to anything. If the end brings me out wrong, ten angels swearing I was right would make no difference." For once, a Lincoln quotation is correctly attributed. Francis Carpenter was a portrait artist who spent six months at the White House painting the president and the Cabinet. Carpenter later published reminiscences that included this saying (Carpenter, 1866). At least two presidents borrowed the sense of the quote. Nixon, speaking of his plan for peace in Vietnam, said, "If it does succeed, what the critics say won't matter. If it does not succeed, anything I say then won't matter" (United States, 1969-1974).

In 1969 Gerald Ford kept in the angels (he was speaking of his pardon of Nixon): "I do believe that right makes might and that if I am wrong, ten angels swearing I was right would make no difference"

(Ford, 1974). Other sources for this quote are Platt (1993) and Harnsberger (1950).

The following aphorisms represent a list of ten points allegedly made by Abraham Lincoln. Is this attribution correct?

1. You cannot bring about prosperity by discouraging thrift.
2. You cannot strengthen the weak by weakening the strong.
3. You cannot help small men up by tearing big men down.
4. You cannot help the poor by destroying the rich.
5. You cannot lift the wage-earner up by pulling the wage-payer down.
6. You cannot keep out of trouble by spending more than your income.
7. You cannot further the brotherhood of man by inciting class hatred.
8. You cannot establish sound social security on borrowed money.
9. You cannot build character and courage by taking away a man's initiative and independence.
10. You cannot help men permanently by doing for them what they could and should do for themselves.

The infamous Lincoln "Ten Points" speech has been conclusively proven to be a hoax. The ten points were copyrighted by a Reverend William J. H. Boetcker in 1916 and took on a life of their own, being picked up by various groups to support their own position. A review of the history of this hoax is in Boller and George (1989). *Respectfully Quoted* (Platt, 1993) says, "Lincoln scholars believe that any connection between Lincoln and the 'Ten Points' is spurious."

Who said, "I believe in an aristocracy, an aristocracy of . . ." followed by various qualities?

Thomas Jefferson said, "There is a natural aristocracy among men. The grounds of this are virtue and talents," which is not exactly the quotation desired (Cappon, 1988). Somerset Maugham said something similar: "I believe in aristocracy, though—if that is the right word, and if a democrat may use it. Not an aristocracy of power, based upon rank and influence, but an aristocracy of the sensitive, the considerate, and the plucky" (Maugham, 1943).

Who said, "Power without responsibility—this has been the lot of the harlot through the ages"?

This is a slight alteration of the original statement. Stanley Baldwin (later Earl Baldwin of Bewdley) said, "Power without responsibility—the prerogative of the harlot through the ages." Baldwin used the words in a speech in which he took the press to task for an attack on him. The words were originally suggested by his cousin Rudyard Kipling (Hyde, 1973).

"I complained that I had no shoes, then I met a man that had no feet." Where did this quote come from?

This story is in *The Gulistan, or Rose Garden,* by the Persian poet Sa'di (1184?-1291), also known as Muslih-al-Din or Muslin-ed-Deen. The earliest translation of his work is by Francis Gladwin:

> I never complained of the vicissitudes of fortune, nor murmured at the ordinances of Heaven, excepting once, when my feet were bare, and I had not the means procuring myself shoes. I entered the great mosque at Cufah with a heavy heart when I beheld a man who had no feet. I offered up praise and Thanksgiving to God for His bounty, and bore with patience the want of shoes. A broiled fowl in the eyes of one who has satisfied his appetite is of less estimation than a leaf of greens on a dish; but to him who hath not the means of procuring food, a broiled turnip is equal to a broiled fowl (Sa'di, 1865).

Another translation in rhyme reads:

> An old man, bound to Mecca, quite a way his sandals wore,
> and on the desert's blistering sand his feet grew very sore,
> He murmured in complaining tone; and in this temper came
> To where, around the Kaaba, pilgrims knelt of every name;
> and there he saw, while pity and remorse his bosom beat,
> An old man, not only wanting shoes but feet!

Oscar Wilde said something like, "I am easily pleased—I am always satisfied with the very best." What was the context?

In a conversation between Wilde and Edgar Saltus, reported in Saltus' book *Oscar Wilde* (Saltus, 1917), Wilde said, "I put a bold face on it. 'Come to my shop,' I said, 'and have dinner with me.'

'Though,' I added, 'I don't know what I can give you.' 'Oh, anything,' Wilde replied, 'Anything, no matter what. I have the simplest tastes. I am always satisfied with the best'" (Wilde, 1946).

Who said, "Education is a companion which no misfortune can depress"?

Originally attributed to Joseph Addison (Kerber, 1968), this is actually by Charles Phillips (1787?-1859), an Irish barrister. In context, the lines read:

> No doubt, you have all personally considered—no doubt, you all personally experienced, that of all the blessings which it has pleased Providence to allow us to cultivate, there is not one which breathes a purer fragrance, or bears an heavenlier aspect than education. It is a companion which no misfortune can depress, no clime destroy, no enemy alienate, no despotism enslave; at home a friend, abroad an introduction, in solitude a solace, in society an ornament, it chastens vice, it guides virtue, it gives at once a grace and government to genius. Without it, what is man?" (Phillips, 1817)

There is a supposed Talmudic quotation reading, "We do not see things as they are. We see things as we are." Robert Kennedy also said something similar. What is the real origin of this?

A book titled *Quotable Women* (Running Press Staff, 1989) attributes this to Anaïs Nin.

A political quotation that sometimes surfaces in election years is the saying that "One useless man is a fool; two are a law firm; and three or more a legislature." Where did this originate?

There is a musical titled *1776*, based on the creation and adoption of the United States Declaration of Independence. It was composed by Sherman Edwards, and Peter Stone wrote the book. In this play, the opening lines in Scene One feature John Adams standing in front of the curtain. Adams says, "I have come to the conclusion that one useless man is called a disgrace, that two are called a law firm, and that three or more become a congress" (Stone, 1970).

Someone who probably would have been happy with the musical in the preceding question once said, "Experience beats in vain on the congenital liberal." Who was this?

The word was "progressive," not "liberal," and it was C. S. Lewis who said, "Experience beats in vain upon a congenital progressive" (Lewis, 1954).

Who said, "Nothing is easier than spending the public money"?

Calvin Coolidge is supposed to have said, "Nothing is easier than spending the public money. It does not appear to belong to anybody. The temptation is overwhelming to bestow it on somebody" (Radford, 1978). Long before Coolidge, similar sentiments were uttered by Thomas Jefferson and John Randolph. Jefferson said, "The same prudence which in private life would forbid our paying our own money for unexplained projects, forbids it in the dispensation of the public moneys" (Platt, 1993).

Randolph said, "That most delicious of all privileges—spending other people's money" (Platt, 1993).

One of the most famous misattributed quotes in history is the saying often referred to as the "Socrates" or "Hitler" quote. The following words appear in various pamphlets, broadsides, etc., usually ending with "Hitler, 1935" (or another date) or "Socrates" (with some B.C. date). "The children now love luxury; they have bad manners, contempt for authority; they show discourtesy for elders and love chatter in place of exercise. Children are now tyrants, not the servants of their households."

Unfortunately, when this is attributed to Socrates, the dates given do not match his dates at all. However, Isocrates (in *Areopagiticus*) has several similar lines: "To contradict one's elders or to be impudent to them was then considered more reprehensible than it is nowadays to sin against one's parents" (Genner, 1928). A complete copy of the quotation is in *Quotable Quotes in Education* (Kerber, 1968).

This is allied to (or confused with) a supposed Hitler quotation to the effect that "The streets of our country are in turmoil. The universities are filled with students rebelling and rioting. . . . We need law and order." The attribution is a speech Hitler made in Hamburg in 1932. The "Trade Winds" column in the *Saturday Review* (Beatty, 1960) attributed this to Adolph Hitler. When Beatty was asked for a source, he researched the question. It turned out that there was no available confirmation. This did not prevent such orators as Senator Edmund Muskie and Justice William O. Douglas from using the "Hitler" quote. *They Never Said It* (Boller and George, 1989) noted:

> The Hitler quote is an obvious fake. The only students rebelling and rioting in Germany in 1932, as the philosopher Sidney Hook has pointed out, were Nazi students protesting against the presence of Jewish professors on the university faculties. And the candidate for law and order in Germany in 1932 was not Hitler, but Field Marshall Paul von Hindenberg.

James Dean: Live Fast, Die Young (the movie) was released in 1998 and a made-for-television special movie about the actor came out in 2001. A saying attributed to James Dean was, "Live fast, die young, and leave a good-looking corpse." Did Dean make this up?

No, the lines are a bit older than James Dean. These lines were spoken by John Derek, playing Nick Romano, in the movie version of Willard Motley's *Knock on Any Door* (Green, 1982). In the book, Nick said, "Live fast, die young and have a good-looking corpse" (p. 157 of the Appleton-Century-Crofts edition). Toward the end of the book, as Romano was in the electric chair, Motley wrote:

> The show was over. You don't have to pretend any more now. All caught up. . . . A kid in an electric chair all caught up. Life had been fast. Death had come young. The good-looking corpse would be carried by its arms and legs to a slab in the autopsy room. (Motley, 1947)

What is the source of "I would rather be ashes than dust; I would rather my spark burn out in a brilliant flame"?

This comment was made by Jack London. He went on to say, "I would not waste my days in trying to prolong them. I shall use my time" (London, 1968).

What fanatic fisherman, at some point in his life, has not seen or even used the line, "God does not deduct from man's allotted span the time spent fishing"? A similar sentiment has been expressed about sailing. Fishing being no province solely of

Western religions, the phrase is also quoted as "Allah does not de-duct. . . ." What brilliant soul first thought of this justification?

Supposedly this is a Babylonian proverb (Tripp, 1970). Herbert Hoover used these lines in a book of reflections about fishing. Hoover wrote, "there is said to be a table of 2000 B.C. which says: 'The Gods do not subtract from the allotted span of men's lives the hours spent in fishing' " (Hoover, 1963).

Among the most recurrent quotations are those which "define" a society. The most popular quotations take on a life of their own and are adopted, adapted, and rephrased by many. Is there any aboriginal source for this type of saying?

At least seven versions of this type of popular saying are known, but there is no certainty about who wrote any original saying or when it originated. Attorney General Ramsey Clark, in a keynote address to the American Correctional Association, said, "There are few better measures of the concern a society has for its individual members and its own well being than the way it handles its criminals" (Clark, 1968). Senator Hubert Horatio Humphrey (1977), in remarks at the dedication of the HEW building, said:

> It was once said that the moral test of government is how that government treats those who are in the dawn of life, the children; those who are in the twilight of life, the elderly; and others who are in the shadows of life—the sick, the needy and handicapped.

William Gladstone had this version attributed to him: "Show me the manner in which a nation or a community cares for its dead. I will measure exactly the sympathies of its people, their respect for the laws of the land, and their loyalty to high ideas" (*American Cemetery,* 1938). Sir John MacDonell, writing of Michael Servetus' trial, said:

> There is no accepted test of civilization. It is not wealth, or the degree of comfort, or the average duration of life, or the increase of knowledge. All such tests would be disputed. In default of any other measure, may it not be suggested that as good a measure as any is the degree to which justice is carried out, the degree to which men are sensitive as to wrong-doing and desirous to right it. If that be the test, a trial such as that of Servetus is a trial of the people among whom it takes place, and his condemnation is theirs also. (MacDonell, 1983)

The Congressional Research Service of the Library of Congress has often been called upon to identify the author of this thought (Platt, 1993). They located a number of variations, some of which follow.

Pearl Buck's version reads ". . . for the test of a civilization is in the way that it cares for its helpless members."

Churchill's use of the phrase was "Nothing can be more abhorrent to democracy than to imprison a person or keep him in prison because he is unpopular. This is really the test of civilization."

Dostoyevsky is supposed to have said, "The degree of civilization in a society can be judged by entering its prisons."

Toynbee, according to a message to Congress from John F. Kennedy, concluded that a society's quality and durability can best be measured "by the respect and care given its elderly citizens."

Where can I find the famous "Chief Seattle" speech?
This speech is discussed at length by Rudolph Kaiser (1987). There are at least four versions of Chief Sealth's words:

1. Dr. Henry A. Smith's account, published in the *Seattle Sunday Star* October 29, 1887, and possibly written from notes he made thirty-three years earlier when he heard the speech on Main Street in Seattle (Smith, 1887).
2. William Arrowsmith's version published in *Arion* (1969) and the *American Poetry Review* (1975).
3. Ted Perry, who rewrote the Arrowsmith version in 1970-1971 for a script for a film titled *Home,* says the speech is fictitious and he probably shouldn't have used Chief Seattle's name. However, this is the version circulated most often and tends to be the one asked for at library reference desks.
4. A version exhibited in the U.S. pavilion of the Spokane Expo 1974, based on Perry's version, but with an enlarged poetic style.

Where did these lines originate: "We have not inherited the earth from our ancestors. We are borrowing it from our children"?
Often attributed to Emerson, definitive proof was never produced for "The Exchange." One source, the *American Review of Canadian Studies,* claims this is a Haida Indian proverb (Keller, 1990).

Where did this saying originate? "Any man who is not a socialist at twenty has no heart; any man who is still a socialist at forty has no head."

This appears to be an approximate translation (with an age change) of a remark by Georges Clemenceau. Clemenceau substituted *socialiste* for *republicain* in adapting an earlier observation of François Guizot, historian and statesman under Louis Philippe. Guizot's original statement was *"N' être pas republicain à vingt ans est prevue d'un manqué de coeur; l' être après trente ans est prevue d'un manqué de tête."* The translation is, "Not to be a republican at twenty is proof of want of heart; to be one at thirty is proof of want of head" (Benham, 1924).

John Kennedy used the phrase, "the only thing necessary for evil to triumph in the world is for good men to do nothing" in a speech. Later, in an election campaign, it was used as a "get out the vote" slogan.

Although standard quotation dictionaries attribute this to Edmund Burke, it has never been found in his works (Platt, 1993). It may be a paraphrase of "When bad men combine, the good must associate; else they will fall one by one, an unpitied sacrifice in a contemptible struggle" in *Thoughts on the Causes of the Present Discontents* (Bartlett, 1980). William Safire explored the confusing origin of this saying in a *New York Times* column (Safire, 1980). Safire wrote: "The only thing necessary for the triumph of misquotation is for wiseguys to do nothing. Unless some Burkian scholar . . . [provides a] genuine citation, that chunk of concentrated wisdom directed to 'good men' is declared counterfeit."

The sentiment is close to something Plato said: "The penalty good men pay for indifference to public affairs is to be ruled by evil men" (Platt, 1993).

Very appropriately for a book such as this, an "Exchange" reader once wanted to know the source of "The world of books is the most remarkable creation of man."

These thoughts appeared in a book by Clarence Day.

> The world of books is the most remarkable creation of man. Nothing else that he builds ever lasts. Monuments fall; nations perish; civilizations grow old and die out; and, after an era of darkness, new races build others. But in the world of books are

volumes that have seen this happen again and again, and yet live on, still young, still as fresh as the day they were written, still telling men's hearts of the hearts of men centuries dead. (Day, 1920)

Who produced the somewhat muddled thought, "How do I know what I think until I write it?"

W. H. Auden, in the "Squares in the Oblongs" section of *Poets at Work* (Arnheim, 1948), includes these words: "How can I know what I think till I see what I say?" The words are in italics with no suggestion as to whether this is for emphasis or whether Auden was paraphrasing.

In the movie *IQ*, reference was made to Albert Einstein saying that "heaven was like a library." Did Einstein really say this?

This quote probably comes from something that Jorge Luis Borges once said. Borges commented, "I have always imagined that Paradise will be a kind of library" (Byrnes, 1982).

George Lyttelton, in *The Lyttelton Hart-Davis Letters,* said, "Seared is of course my heart, but unsubdued shall be my appetite for food." A library user wanted to know if there was an earlier source for this quotation.

These lines are found toward the end (lines 111 and 112) of a poem titled "Beer" in *The English Poems of Charles Stuart Calverley* (Spear, 1974).

What is the source of ". . . and the Lion shall lie down with the Lamb"?

This is not the way the sentiment is worded in Isaiah 11:6, which reads, "The wolf also shall dwell with the lamb, and the leopard shall lie down with the kid; and the calf and the young lion and the fatling together; and a little child shall lead them."

Percy Shelley (1812) may have been the one who got his animals confused, since he wrote, "In the dimness of whose distance, I behold the lion lay down with the lamb and the infant play with the basilisk." Some of the confusion about which animal was lying down with which may have come from Edward Hicks' painting, *The Peaceable Kingdom* (Larkin, 1949).

What is the source of "You can kill a flock of sheep with incantations provided you give them arsenic first"?

Voltaire said, "It is unquestionable that certain words and ceremonies will effectually destroy a flock of sheep, if administered with a sufficient portion of arsenic" (Morley, 1901).

Did Carl Jung say, "Hurry is of the Devil"?

The expression "Haste is of the Devil" appears in several quotation dictionaries, but not with an attribution to Jung (Mencken, 1942; Stevenson, 1934). Stevenson says, "Alleged to be from the Koran but not found."

It is not exactly a quotation, but there is a story to this effect: A woman says to a man, "What kind of woman do you think I am?" The man replies, "We've already established that, Madam. Now we're simply determining the price." What is the source?

This is an apocryphal story attributed to George Bernard Shaw. Shaw is said to have asked a lady at dinner one night if she would go to bed with him for 1,000 pounds. The lady hesitated but finally agreed, so Shaw asked if she would do the same for one pound. "Certainly not!" objected the lady. "What do you take me for?" "We have already settled that," said Shaw. "What we are trying to find out now is the price" (Esar, 1978).

Chapter 6

There Will Always
Be Reference Librarians

In a library periodical, a librarian discussed his frustration with "stupid questions" (Plaiss, 1985). Judging from the mail response, readers weren't sure whether the article was intended as humor or as a comment from a somewhat burned-out librarian. In either case, those of us who work at a reference desk, particularly a busy one, probably saw at least a small measure of our own reality in the author's comments.

Standing behind a desk labeled "Information" or "Reference," offering to all comers "The Answer" to their question—dealing with wildly varying subjects as frequently as every three or four minutes—is a stressful occupation. Obviously there are enough psychic rewards in exposing ourselves to this barrage of demands to keep most of us in the profession. However, it is inevitable that the constant pressure of responding accurately and quickly to the demands made on us can lead to some periods of frustration—particularly by the end of the week, when the article probably was written.

It is very important to keep reminding ourselves that the questions we are asked do not belong to us—they belong to the questioner. We *cannot* classify them as stupid—they are not our questions to classify. All we can do is try to answer them to the best of our ability. It is very unlikely the person asking the question thinks it's stupid—even while saying, "I know this is a dumb question, but . . ."

I think it is a healthy exercise to put yourself in the patron's place every now and then. Imagine the nerve it must take to approach a total stranger to ask a question about something that really matters to you. If the question does sound stupid—if someone asks, "Is this the reference desk?" immediately after you have answered the phone "John Jones, reference desk, can I help you?"—then empathize, empathize,

empathize. Maybe the caller is so wrapped up in formulating a question that he or she did not even hear your stock phone response.

Pinned down by a day of "Where's that green book that finds articles for you?" and moaning for release, you may wonder why you became a reference librarian—and if you are really needed. Take comfort—there will always be a need for reference librarians. We play a role in meeting one of the most basic human needs, the need to wonder. This need was present long before reference librarians existed, but now that at least some of the public knows about libraries, librarians will be there to relieve that constant urge to know, to seek answers, and, one hopes, to continue providing answers.

Reference librarianship is as much art as science. The computer groupies in our profession may well develop "expert systems" that can do some of the tasks of a good reference librarian. Even now computers can do marvelous things to help find answers. However, until it is possible to program a sense of empathy and wonder into an expert system, it is difficult for me to see the replacement of human by machine in this field.

Reference work, by its very nature, often is reactive rather than proactive. Occasionally we may find answers to questions that have not yet been asked and put them away in some "Hard Question" file. I suspect there may be a general reluctance to be very diligent in this area. It is too easy to be pessimistic about the utility of such work. Even with a good indexing system, we tend to wonder about the likelihood of another reference librarian retrieving this ephemeral information at some future date.

From this minimal level of squirreling away bits of information for potential later use to actually calling our users' attention to possible information shortages in their lives is quite a step. I'm sure it is a step taken in some libraries. Perhaps more of us ought to consider this type of information service. It is difficult for the public actively to deal with problems that seem remote from day-to-day life. For example, most literate people are aware of some possible future problems with such things as ozone layer depletion and air pollution. Most Americans do not feel that the actual hazards and necessity for dealing with these issues are very pressing. For one thing, the primary sources of information on such topics for most people are newspapers, popular magazines, and television.

Human nature makes it easy to gloss over this kind of information as "scare tactics" or "headline grabbers." Libraries may be thought of as a source with a bit more credibility. We have lots of information on these problems and other pressing issues. Unfortunately, most sources sit locked up on our shelves waiting for someone to ask a question. Perhaps we ought to take a bit more responsibility for opening up information sources to the public. Selective dissemination of information (SDI) has been around at least as long as I've been working in libraries (a period of time that now extends so far into the past that I hate to mention specifics anymore). It became a hot item when online databases came into fashion in the 1970s, particularly in academic and special libraries. If one simply stretches the definition a bit, the medieval monk who kept an eye out for special manuscripts for an ecclesiastical superior was practicing SDI. The caretaker in the Alexandrian library who watched out for the special interests of some wealthy Greek noble was practicing SDI. Perhaps one could say that the Egyptian messenger who rushed up to Pharaoh crying, "The Hyksos are coming, the Hyksos are coming," was practicing SDI. In any case, the computer did not invent this concept; it simply made it easier.

Public libraries, at least as far as I am aware, have never actively promoted SDI on any consistent basis. This is too bad, because the newest Web browsers from Microsoft and Netscape offer relatively simple ways proactively to supply information to targeted audiences.

I suspect that just about any public library could identify some special interests of patrons that would benefit from a regular updating service. Just to name a few that come to mind:

- Short lists of new acquisitions in very narrow fields
- A Web page with links to new sites in high-interest areas (such as cancer treatment)
- Virtual book talks or short annotated lists of materials on hot topics
- The library's job page
- Specific areas of interest from the business librarian
- Student information on projects such as history or science fairs
- Recurring library programs
- Basic library PR announcements
- Local government information

Think of it as a "What's New"-type item pushed to subscribers who normally wouldn't check the library's homepage every day. The potential content list is as broad as a library's user base. All it would take (given a preexisting library Web page) is staff with the capability and interest to digest and summarize new material, some publicity, and minimal Web page maintenance. Once a basic structure is created, at least some of this process could very well be automated.

As concerns arise about the future role of reference librarians in a digital world, this human, professional interface between the flow of information and the public seems to be one possible area for some exciting involvement on the part of librarians. It might be a natural way that librarians could become more involved with new technology. It is also a natural way to bring a librarian's talent of organizing and presenting information to bear on the "information explosion."

As one example, the *Chicago Tribune* carried an article by J. E. Ferrell titled "Saving Clean Air from Its Last Gasp" (Ferrell, 1990). The story is about an amendment to the clean-air bill in Congress at the time that "seeks to protect the last reservoir of clean air in the contiguous 48 states." According to the writer, the U.S. National Park Service had found an area about 400 miles in diameter in northeastern Nevada, northwestern Utah, and southern Idaho where the air is still clear enough to see as far as 185 miles. This is apparently the only place left in the country with no major sources of pollution.

The story describes places such as the Grand Canyon where, on some days, visitors "can no longer see the Colorado River at the bottom of the canyon. . . . When the Shenandoah National Park was established in Virginia in 1935, people could make out the Capitol and the Washington Monument 70 miles away." Today the median visibility in the summer in this area is around eleven miles. Some national parks now have ozone warning days in the summer when it is unhealthy for visitors to hike. When my daughter was young, we went camping in some of these parks. It has been a number of years since then, and I did not realize even our parks had gotten this bad.

Unless one personally experiences dramatic changes such as this, it is not easy to feel concern to the point of action. As Santayana said, "Those who cannot remember the past are condemned to repeat it" (Platt, 1993). We do displays in entrances and general browsing areas of our libraries. What would be wrong with being more proactive about displays in our reference rooms featuring current problems and possible solutions as consciousness-raising efforts? However, we do have to remain neutral. We would have to provide information on all sides of these knotty questions. Wouldn't it be a good form of reference outreach to present this type of information for every user instead of waiting for one interested party to ask?

Chapter 7

Poem Fragments

If the reader suspects that the categories in this book are arranged somewhat in order of increasing difficulty of resolution, there is probably some justification for that suspicion. Identifying fragments of poems, often found on tattered pieces of paper that have been carried in some ancestor's wallet or purse for many years, can be exceedingly challenging. When found, however, the psychic reward (and often the feedback from the patron) is correspondingly gratifying.

$$* \quad * \quad *$$

In Chapter 1 we discussed the reason for carving half-moons in outdoor privies. Now to fully cover this somewhat scatological subject, we have a question about a poem dealing with the passing of the outhouse.

"The Passing of the Backhouse" is the most common title for a piece often attributed to James Whitcomb Riley. However, Riley's publisher as well as his close friends and relatives denied Riley's authorship of the poem (Kennedy, 1952). According to the *Chicago Tribune* (1976), the poem was printed in a broadside, leaflet, and a pamphlet titled, "Suppressed Poems by James Whitcomb Riley and Eugene Field." The *Tribune* noted that even though Riley's authorship was denied by friends and relatives, these same people for decades "ignored the fact that the man who wrote 'Little Boy Blue' and 'Wynken, Blynken, and Nod' also enjoyed writing poetry that would make many adults blush." According to Riley's sister-in-law, Julia Wilson Riley, the poem was actually written by Dr. W. C. Cooper, a close friend of Riley (Williamson, 1979).

The first stanza reads:

When memory keeps me company and moves to smiles or tears,
A weather-beaten object looms through the mist of years.
Behind the house and barn it stood, a half-mile or more,
and hurrying feet a path had made, straight to its swinging door.

Of course, if you are intimately involved with the backhouse, the last thing you want to think of is this little ditty: "Big bugs have little bugs on their backs to bite 'em, and little bugs still smaller ones and so on infinitum." Where did this enlightening reminder originate?

The earliest version of these lines appears in Jonathan Swift's *On Poetry* (1773/1958).

If, on Parnassus' Top you sit
You rarely bit, are always bit;
Each poet of inferior Size
On you shall rail and criticize;
. . .
So Nat'ralists observe, a Flea
Hath smaller Fleas that on him prey,
and these have smaller fleas to bite 'em,
and so proceed ad infinitum.

Aside from fleas or bugs, you also do not want "ghosties and ghoulies and long-legged beasties" visiting you. From where do these creatures come?

Usually phrased as a prayer, this is commonly assigned a Scottish origin. One version is called "an old Cornish litany" (Adshead and Duff, 1948), and reads:

From Ghoulies and Ghosties
and long-leggity Beasties,
and all Things that go bump in the Night,
Good Lord deliver us.

A note in *Notes and Queries* (1955) points out that "there seems no justification for associating this with Cornwall, even though it has appeared there on picture post-cards and souvenirs for years."

What is the source of "Where the jam pots grow, Where the jam pots grow, Where the jolly, jelly jam pots grow"?

These lines are the chorus of a poem with musical accompaniment that was written by Laura E. Richards (Werner, 1906-1907). The first verse reads:

> You may talk about your groves,
> Where you wander with your loves,
> You may talk about your moonlit ways that fallen flow;
> I can tell you, if you will,
> of the house upon the hill,
> and the charming little cupboards
> Where the jam pots grow.

Moving on from this odd train of thought to baseball, "The Exchange" was asked to locate a poetic response to "Casey at the Bat," about O'Reilly, the pitcher who struck Casey out.

The author never surfaced, but the poem is included in a booklet distributed by the Fort Pitt Brewing Company (Rowswell, n.d.). The first stanza goes like this:

> There's been a lot of smoking over Casey and his bat,
> and how he didn't win the game and other guff like that;
> They've made some rhymes about him and that sort of swelled his fame,
> But's what's the good of crackin' up the mutt that lost the game?

Further details about Riley and the careers of others associated with the incident can be found in *The Associated Casey at the Bat* (Gardner, 1967).

Where can I find a copy of the poem titled "The Greata Game of Baseball"?

The author is Thomas Augustine Daly, and the correct title is "Da Greata Baseball" (Daly, 1912). The first stanza is:

> Oh! Greata game ees baseball
> For yo'nga 'Merican.
> But, o! my frand, ees not at all
> Da theeng for Dagoman.

It can be found in *Werner's Readings and Recitations* (Werner, 1906-1907).

There is a poem with these remembered lines: "There's one of me that's humble for sins / and one that unrepentant sits and grins . . ." What is the source and full text of this poem?

There are several poems that have very similar lines. One is by Edward Martin (1914) and reads:

> Within my earthly temple there's a crowd
> There's one that's humble, one that's proud.
> There's one that's broken-hearted for his sins,
> and one that unrepentant, sits and grins.
> There's one that loves his neighbors as himself,
> and one that cares for naught but fame and pelf.
> From such perplexing care I would be free.

On the other hand, Edward Sanford White wrote a very similar poem titled "My Name Is Legion," with an alternate title, "Which Is Me?" White was the founder of the *Harvard Lampoon* and first editor of *Life*. His poem differs in a few words and punctuation, as well as having a different next-to-last line: "From much corroding care I should be free" (Blietz, 1982).

Where can one find a copy of a poem titled "The Self-Appointed Bastard"?

Attributed to Ogden Nash, but not located specifically, some lines read (Scheetz, 1988):

> On a lonely Southern chain gang,
> On a dusty Southern road,
> My late lamented pappy
> Made his permanent abode.
> Some were there for stealing,
> But my daddy's only fault
> Was an overwhelming tendency
> For criminal assault.

Where can I find a copy of "The Lawyer's Prayer," possibly by Sir Thomas More?

"The Sainted More" is the way Inspector Grant refers to the revered St. Thomas More in Josephine Tey's *Daughter of Time*. Grant was disgusted with More for perpetrating what even the *Encyclopedia Americana* now refers to as the "Tudor myth" about the alleged villany of Richard III. Perhaps it is fitting that More, the patron saint of lawyers, has several different, conflicting prayers associated with his name (McNamara, 1967; *Ragbag of Legal Quotations,* 1960). One version reads:

> Give me the grace Good Lord,
> To set the world at naught;
> To set my mind fast upon Thee
> and not to hang upon men's mouths.
> To be content to be Solitary.
> Not to long for worldly company
> But utterly to cast off the world
> and rid my mind of the business thereof.

A second version is longer. Here are the first two paragraphs and the close:

> St. Thomas More, be our advocate and counsel before the Divine tribunal that alone is without error.
>
> Bespeak for us the wisdom to apply the precepts of God's eternal law to the problems of our daily practice.
> . . .
> Pray that we may spurn false oaths and live as you did, faithful to our trusts as members of the Bar, even though by doing so we may be called upon to sacrifice our lives as you sacrificed yours.
>
> These things seek for us to the merits of Jesus Christ, Our Lord, Amen.

A final version, which supposedly originated with Senator Sam Ervin, reads "Stir up much strife amongst the people, Lord, lest thy servant perish" (Hay, 1989).

Where can a copy of a poem titled "The Man in the Glass" be found?

The correct title is "The Guy in the Glass," and it is by Dale Wimbrow (*American Magazine*, 1934), although some copies carry the title "The Man in the Mirror." The poem begins:

> When you get what you want in your struggle for pelf,
> and the world makes you King for a day,
> Then go to the mirror and look at yourself,
> and see what that guy has to say.

It ends with these lines:

> You can fool the whole world down the pathway of years,
> and get pats on the back as you pass,
> But your final reward will be heartaches and tears
> If you've cheated the guy in the glass.

Where can I find a copy of the poem "The Box"?

This antiwar poem is by Kenneth Lascelles. During the 1960s and 1970s it was read on programs such as *The Smothers Brothers Comedy Hour* and was recorded on a John Denver album, *Poems, Prayers and Promises* (Denver, 1971). It also was published as a book (Lascelles, 1974). The first and last stanzas are:

> Once upon a time in the land of hush-a-bye,
> Around about the wondrous days of yore,
> They came across a sort of box
> Bound up with chains and locked with locks
> and labeled "Kindly do not touch, it's war."
> . . .
> Well that's the way it all appears
> 'Cos its been bouncing round for years and years
> In spite of all the wisdom wizzed
> Since those wondrous days of yore,
> And the time they came across that box
> Bound up with chains and locked with locks
> And labeled, "Kindly do not touch, it's war."

Now for a bit of romance, who wrote the following bit of love poetry?

> **I do believe that God above created you for me to love.**
> **He picked you out from all the rest,**
> **Because He knew I love you best.**

The lines closely resemble the third stanza of "Tell Me Why," a song associated with the campus tradition of dormitory and sorority candle lightings:

> The song was sung while a candle was passed around a circle of women (who did not know to whom the candle belonged) until it was blown out by the owner, thereby announcing her recent engagement. Usually, the engagement ring was attached to the candle in some way, for all to admire. (Kayes, 1977)

The full text is in Best and Best (1967), and the stanza after the one quoted above is:

> Because God made the stars to shine
> Because God made the ivy twine,
> Because God made the sky so blue,
> Because God made you, that's why I love you.

Another poem partially remembered from early school days was one that included these lines:

> **If you're not there on Judgment Day**
> **I'll know you went the other way.**
> **I'll give the angels back their wings,**
> **Their golden harp, and other things.**
> **and to show what I would do,**
> **I'd even go to hell for you.**

While no specific author ever surfaced, several possible versions were offered. One writer who provided the version below said the poem was something passed around in junior high school days (Nelson, 1979). The missing lines, which precede the remembered ones, are:

> I had a heart and it was true,
> But now it's gone from me to you.
> Take care of it as I have done,
> For you have two and I have none.
> When I get to Heaven and you're not there,
> I'll write your name on the golden stair,
> To let the angels know and see
> How my darling I love thee.

Where can one find a poem by Clarence Darrow that includes these lines?

> **So I be written in the book of love**
> **I do not care about that book above,**
> **Erase my name or write it as you will,**
> **So I be written in the book of love.**

David W. Rintels based the television program in which Henry Fonda recited these lines from a play, which in turn was based on *Clarence Darrow for the Defense* (Stone, 1941). Clarence Darrow did write a book titled *A Persian Pearl,* which was published in 1889 and may contain the sought-for lines. There is a similar quatrain from Omar Khayyam in the *Library of the World's Best Literature* (1896) that reads:

> Hearts with the light of love illuminated well
> Whether in mosque or synagogue they dwell
> Have their names written in the book of love,
> Unvex'd by hopes of heaven or fears of hell.

Who wrote the poem that begins "Do not stand by my grave and weep"? Other lines include: "I am a diamond glint on snow, I am the sunlight on rippled grain, I am the gentle autumn rain."

Mary E. Frye wrote this poem in 1932 to comfort a friend whose mother had died. Her friend's mother had lived in Germany, but because of Hitler's rise to power, she had urged her daughter not to come. The other woman said to Mary, "What hurts the worst is that I never got to stand by my mother's grave and shed a tear."

The poem, signed "Anonymous," made its way into sympathy cards, funeral services, and a movie. In 1983 Frye still kept copies to fill requests from all over the world. She received correspondence from many people who have been comforted by the words. A story about her life appeared in her local newspaper in Dundalk, Maryland (Blatchford, 1984). Some Web sites identify Frye as the author with a date of 1932, while others attribute the poem to "Anonymous."

An Ann Landers column once attributed the poem to the Makah Indians, but as an "Exchange" reader pointed out, the Makahs do not have snow, fields of grain, or gentle autumn rains—they have heavy autumn rains. Furthermore, Native American traditions seldom favor the "I am still with you" approach of this poem but rather like to get the spirit moving away from the living as quickly as possible.

What is the full text of the poem that begins, "If any little word of mine"?

It took thirty-five years to find the answer to this—twenty years searching by the patron and fifteen years after it appeared in "The Exchange." The source is "The Little Word." The author is unknown. The poem is in *Poetry Worth Remembering* (Watson, 1986). The poem also was set to music, and a copy can be found in *The New Advent Hymnal* (1952). In this latter source, the authors are given as A. N. O. and F. E. B. with D. S. Hakes as composer. F. E. B. was Franklin E. Belden (1858-1945), a prominent Seventh-Day Adventist song writer (*Seventh-Day Adventist Encyclopedia,* 1976), but A. N. O. is unknown. Here is the first stanza:

> If any little word of mine
> May make a life the brighter,
> If any little song of mine
> May make a heart the lighter,
> God help me speak the little word,
> And take my bit of singing,
> And drop it in some lovely vale
> To set the echoes ringing.

What are the lines of the poem titled "The Apache Prayer"?
This beautiful poem reads:

> Now you will feel no rain
> for you will be shelter to the other.
> Now you will feel no cold
> for you will be warmth to the other.
> Now there is no more loneliness
> for each of you will be companion to the other.
> Go now to your dwelling place
> To enter into the days of your togetherness
> and may your days be good, and long upon the earth.

The other side of the coin may be inherent in the request for a poem with the line, "If you love somebody set them free."
The text is in liner notes for an album that has a song with the same title. The album is by Sting (1985), and the title is *The Dream of the Blue Turtles,* A & M Records, SP-3750. It was attributed to Fritz Perls, but the source for this was a "keychain."

There is a religious poem about the sand dollar. What is this poem?
The poem is titled "The Legend of the Sand Dollar." Several versions are extant. The following lines turn up frequently on Web sites (sometimes credited to the Stumpers-L listserv):

> There's a pretty little legend
> That I would like to tell
> of the birth and death of Jesus
> Found in this lowly shell.
> If you examine closely,
> You'll see that you find here
> Four nail holes and a fifth one
> Made by a Roman's spear.
> On one side the Easter lily,
> Its center is the star
> That appeared unto the shepherds
> and led them from afar.
> The Christmas poinsettia,
> Etched on the other side

Reminds us of His birthday,
Our happy Christmastide.
Now break the center open,
and here you will release
The five white doves awaiting
To spread good will and peace.
This simple little symbol,
Christ left for you and me
To help us spread His Gospel
Through all eternity. (Anonymous)

The following lines are on an oil painting (artist unknown, circa 1900s): "and stroll among overshadowing woods of oak—lending in summer from the heats of noon, a whispering shade." What is the source?

Proving once again that "The Exchange" readers can find just about anything, the exact poem, with the single word change of "beech" rather than "oak," is "Beachy Head," by Charlotte Smith (1807).

Where can I find the text of a silly poem that begins "The bare-foot boy with shoes on sat laying on the burning deck."

Although the boy is not barefoot, he is standing on a burning deck (Cole, 1959). The first two stanzas read:

The boy stood on the burning deck,
His fleece was white as snow;
He stuck a feather in his hat,
John Anderson, my Jo!
"Come back, come back," he cried in grief,
From India's coral strands,
The frost is on the pumpkin and
The village smithy stands. (Anonymous)

Another version comes from a song by Bradley Kincaid and his Kentucky Mountain Boys and is titled "Ain't We Crazy" (Herman, 1993).

It was midnight on the ocean—not a streetcar was in sight,
and the sun was shining bright for it rained all day last night.

Twas a summer night in winter and the rain was snowing fast,
and a bare-footed boy with boots on stood sitting on the grass.

A third alternative, which begins with the above lines but departs in the succeeding verses, can be found in a book titled *Rhymes of the Playground* (n.d.).

Where can one find a copy of the poem "A Trip to Morrow"?

Besides an old Kingston Trio recording, *String Along* (Capitol T1407), this can be found in *Sing Song Scuppernong* (Hardendorff, 1974) and *Poems Teachers Ask for: Book One* (1925).

What words rhyme with "orange"?

Ogden Nash, in "A Brief Guide to Rhyming," has one stanza that reads: "I was once slapped by a young lady named Miss Goringe / and the only reason I was looking at her that way, / She represented a rhyme for orange" (Nash, 1957).

Poet Arthur Guiterman (Lederer, 1994) wrote:

> In Sparkhill buried lies a man of mark
> Who brought the Obelisk to Central Park,
> Redoubtable Commander H. H. Goringe,
> Whose name supplies the long-sought rhyme for orange.

H. H. Gorringe, by the way, was Henry Honeychurch Gorringe, who oversaw the transport of Cleopatra's Needle to New York's Central Park.

Probably every librarian, upon receiving yet another interminable questionnaire, would benefit from reading the full text of the following poem:

> **Thou shalt not answer questionnaires**
> **Or quizzes upon World Affairs**
> **Nor with compliance**
> **Take any test. Thou shalt not sit**
> **With statisticians, nor commit**
> **A social science.**

W. H. Auden penned these lines in the twenty-seventh stanza of his Phi Beta Kappa poem, titled "Under Which Lyre: A Reactionary Tract for the Times" (Auden, 1966).

There is a poem about state capitals and rivers that includes lines such as "Maine, Augusta on the Kennebec," and "New Hampshire, Concord on the Merrimac." What is the title and who wrote this?

In his book *The Winooski,* Hill (1949) says, "thousands of New England school children learned their state capitals" by memorizing this poem. One "Exchange" reader suggested that a book titled *The Poetical Geography* (Van Waters, 1863) might contain the desired poem.

What is the full text of the poem about "humility, the fairest flower"? Remembered lines run: "Humility, the fairest flower that grew in Eden, / The first that died. / It is so frail that it dare not look upon itself."

Caroline Fry (Mrs. Caroline Fry Wilson) (1787-1846) wrote something with lines very like the above in a poem titled "Humility." At the end of the poem, these lines are found (Fry, 1822):

> Humility! the loveliest, sweetest flower
> That bloomed in Paradise,
> and the first that died,
> has rarely blossom'd since on mortal soil.
> It is so frail, so delicate a thing,
> T'is gone if it but look upon itself;
> and she who ventures to esteem it hers
> Proves by that single thought she has it not.

There is a poem by a contemporary American or English poet, about the hospital birth of a first son, who is a Mongoloid. Only the first two lines are remembered: "'Let it be a son,' he said. / 'Your son is a Mongol,' he said." What is the title?

A Familiar Tree, by Jon Stallworthy (1978) could contain the desired poem. A poem in this book called "The Almond Tree" relates the birth of a retarded son.

What are the words of a poem that includes a line about "those tiny fingers"?

Probably one of the most maudlin rhymes to appear in "The Exchange," one version runs:

> If I knew those tiny fingers
> Pressed against the window pane
> Should be cold and stiff tomorrow
> Never trouble us again.
> Would the marks of baby fingers
> Fret us as they do now?

In another version, the second verse reads:

> Would the bright eyes of our darling
> Catch the frown upon our brow
> Would the print of baby fingers
> Vex as they do now?

Continuing in this somewhat somber tone, who penned these depressing lines?

> **Good people, do you love your lives?**
> **This is a knife like other knives . . .**
> **I need but stick it in my breast**
> **and all you folk will die.**

This is a paraphrase of a poem by A. E. Housman (1945). The correct lines are:

> Good creatures, do you love your lives
> and have you ears for sense?
> Here is a knife like other knives,
> That cost me eighteen pence.
> I need but stick it in my heart
> and down will come the sky,
> and earth's foundations will depart
> and all you folk will die.

In the same vein, one patron wanted the poem that begins, "I thought of a mound in sweet Auburn."

These lines are from the fifth stanza of "First Snowfall," by James Lowell (1925). Auburn refers to the Mt. Auburn Cemetery in Cambridge, Massachusetts (Senghas, 1976). The full stanza reads:

> I thought of a mound in sweet Auburn
> Where a little headstone stood;
> How the flakes were folding it gently,
> As did robins the babes in the wood.

What is the source of the poem with these lines? "For some men die by shrapnel, / and some go down in flames, / But most men die in little games."

The poem is titled "The Night They Burned Shanghai" by Robert D. Abrahams (1939) and appeared in *The Saturday Evening Post*. The first two lines above are correct, but the rest of this stanza reads: "But most men perish inch by inch / In play at little games."

In one of the bedrooms in the house where Lizzie Borden lived, a poem was carved into the mahogany lintel above the fireplace. The lines read:

> **and old time friends and twilight plays**
> **and starry nights and sunny days**
> **Come trooping up the misty way**
> **when my fire burns low.**

The carving is referred to in *Lizzie* (Spiering, 1984). What is the origin of this poem?

Those who celebrate Lizzie Borden Liberation Day (August 4) might be interested to learn that Ms. Borden was very fond of the poetry of Scotsman Allan Cunningham (Kent, 1992). Although "The Exchange" never identified this poem with certainty, it could be one titled, "In-my-ain-at-hame Countrie."

The memory of parental recitations and exhortations sometimes leads to puzzling reference questions at the local library. In this case, a patron's father used to recite the words to something

called "The Romance of the Blue Velvet Band." When the local resources were exhausted, "The Exchange" was asked to locate the original.

This comes from a ballad/folk song titled "The Blue Velvet Band." According to tradition, John (Jack) Leonard wrote it while he was in San Quentin prison. The rather lengthy rhyme tells of his seduction to a life of crime by "the girl with the blue velvet band," who then threw him over for a policeman, or "copper." She ends up, naturally enough, in potter's field. One version can be found in *Weep Some More, My Lady* (Spaeth, 1927).

A different version, titled "The Black Velvet Band," appears on *Bad Lads and Hard Cases,* sung by Ewan McColl (n.d.). This version was a popular pub song among farm workers in the 1920s. Perhaps the original source was "The Maid with the Bonny Brown Hair," which dates at least to the early 1800s, when it was transformed in England or Ireland into "The Black Velvet Band." It includes a reference to "transportation" to Van Diemen's Land (Australia), which does put it in the early part of the nineteenth century. From Australia, gold miners moving to the fields of California brought it to the United States. The last named version can be found in *Irish Street Ballads* by Colm O'Lachlainn (1960). The notes in this source indicate that it was collected from a fisherman in Ardglass in 1913.

Another partly remembered poem had to do with a deer chasing something or being chased, leaping over a stream, and "breaking wind." What is the title of this scatological work?

This is probably from the second stanza of the anonymous "Sumer Is Icumen In," also called "The Cuckoo Song" (not particularly noted in people's minds as being scatological) which reads, "Awe bleteh after lomb, lhouth after calve cu; Bulluc sterteth, bucke verteth, Murie sing cuccu" (*New Oxford,* 1972). *The Explicator Cyclopedia* (1966) has a fascinating discussion of whether "verteth" meant "breaking wind" or something else.

There is a poem about a white-footed deer, worshiped by Indians. What is the title?

This poem is by W. C. Bryant and is titled "The White-Footed Deer" (*Poems Teachers Ask For: Book One,* 1925).

Where can one find a dramatic reading or poem beginning, "Sing me a song, my Alice." The reading/poem ends with "Home, home, sweet, sweet home."

Memory being the elusive element that it is, it is at least possible this might be a poem by Anna Seward. The poem opens with "Sweet Alice" and ends with "Home, My Happy Home." It is supposed to be in a magazine named *Little Corporal* (1872).

Who wrote the poem with these lines: "There was an old, old, old, old lady, / and a boy who was half past three"?

The author was Henry Cuyler Bunner, and the poem is "One, Two, Three." (Bunner, 1897; *Poems Teachers Ask For: Book One,* 1925; Stevenson, 1953).

> It was an old, old, old, old lady,
> and a boy that was half-past three;
> and the way they played together
> Was beautiful to see.

The last stanza is:

> and they had never stirred from their places
> Right under the maple tree—
> This old, old, old, old lady
> and the boy with the lame little knee—
> This dear, dear, dear old lady,
> and the boy who was half-past three.

Where can I find a poem with the title "Children Live What They Learn"?

The correct title for this poem is "Children Learn What They Live." The author is Dorothy Law Nolte (Adler, 1974). The first four lines are:

> If a child lives with criticism
> He learns to condemn.
> If a child lives with hostility
> He learns to fight.

Another version of these thoughts is in a poem by Ronald Russell, titled "Lessons from Life" (Russell, 1975). This poem begins:

> A child that lives with ridicule learns to be timid,
> A child that lives with criticism learns to condemn,
> A child that lives with distrust learns to be deceitful.
> A child that lives with antagonism learns to be hostile.

There is a cute children's poem about putting things off . . . procrastinating. What is the title?
The closest answer received by "The Exchange" was an untitled poem by Richard LeGallienne (Arbuthnot and Root, 1968). The first stanza goes:

> I meant to do my work to-day—
> But a brown bird sang in the apple tree,
> and a butterfly flitted across the field,
> and all the leaves were calling me.

Who is the author of the famous Stanley Holloway monologue or poem about "Albert and the Lion"?
This was one of twelve "Albert" monologues written by Marriott Edgar and Wolseley Charles in the 1930s and included in the repertoire of Stanley Holloway—being spoken often in appearances and on recordings. A number of these were recorded by Columbia in England and reissued in the United States on Angel 65019 in 1955. Numerous sources for these monologues exist, for example, Marshall (1979, 1981).

There is a poem about the Magna Carta that includes a line about King John being out in a boat, "'aving some shrimps wi' 'is tea." Where can a copy be found?
This is another monologue by Marriott Edgar that was popularized by Stanley Holloway. The Marshall source mentioned previously includes a copy.

What are the words of a poem by Clemence Dane titled "The [or This] Welcoming Land"?
This poem was recited by Noël Coward (1943) on the reverse side of his record *Don't Let's Be Beastly to the Germans*. The closing line

is: "This sceptered isle, this welcoming land." The sceptered isle part, of course, is from *Richard II*.

What is the title of the long, narrative poem about George Nidever in which he saves the life of a young boy attacked by a grizzly bear?

This poem, titled "George Nidiver," can be found in *Parnassus* (Emerson, 1875) and *The Household Book of Poetry* (Dana, 1970). Here are the first and last stanzas:

> Men have done brave deeds,
> and bards have sung them well;
> I of good George Nidiver
> Now the tale will tell.
>
> . . .
>
> But sure that rifle's aim,
> Swift choice of generous part,
> Showed in his passing gleam
> The depths of a brave heart. (Anonymous)

A certain Deacon Jones tried to convince his parishioners that playing baseball on Sunday to raise money for repairing the church roof was permissible, since baseball is mentioned throughout the Bible. He used a poem to illustrate this. What was the poem?

Sadly, the only fragment "The Exchange" ever got for this poem was the following lines:

> Eve stole first and Adam stole second;
> St. Peter umpired the game.
> Rebekah went to the well with a pitcher,
> and Ruth in the field won fame.

Various Web pages now carry the following:

> In the Big Inning, Eve stole first, Adam stole second.
> Cain struck out Abel, and the Prodigal Son came home.
> The Giants and the Angels were rained out.

What is the source of "From the ferry to Van Ness / It's a godforsaken mess," a bit of doggerel about the San Francisco Fire of 1906?

These lines are from the second stanza of "The Damndest Finest Ruins" by Lawrence Harris (Jackson, 1952).

Bully ruins—ruins and wall—through the night I've heard you call
Sort of sorry for each other 'cause you had to burn and fall,
From the Ferries to Van Ness you're a God-forsaken mess,
But the damndest finest ruins—nothin' more or nothin' less.

Life has been compared to a game of cards in a poem. What is the title of the poem?

There is a poem titled "Whist" by Eugene Fitch Ware whose second stanza begins:

> Life is a game of whist.
> From unseen sources
> The cards are shuffled,
> and the cards are dealt.

A copy can be found in *Poems That Live Forever* (Felleman, 1965). "The Exchange" also received an unattributed copy of a poem titled, "Life Is But a Game of Cards," which begins (Gosik, 1996):

Life is but a game of cards which each one has to learn,
Each shuffles, cuts and deals a pack, and each a trump doth turn,
Some hold a high card at the top, while others turn a low,
Some hold a hand quite full of trumps, while others none can show.

There is a parody of John Masefield's "I Must Go Down to the Seas Again." Where can a copy be found?

When Mrs. John Masefield and her husband, the author of "Sea Fever"—"I must go down to the seas again," etc.—arrived on a liner, she said to a reporter, "It was too uppy-downy and Mr. Masefield was ill." The first stanza of a parody by Arthur Guiterman reads (White, 1941):

I must go down to the seas again, where the billows romp and reel,
So all I ask is a large ship that rides on an even keel,

and a mild breeze and a broad deck with a slight list to leeward,
and a clean chair in a snug nook and a nice, kind steward.

An elderly patron was looking for a poem that her father recited when she was a young girl. The refrain was, "A cup of water, a glass of wine." The idea is that one of these brings no pain, while the other brings ruination and causes grief in the house.

This might be something called "The Two Glasses" by Ella Wheeler Wilcox (1850-1919). Although the line itself does not appear in this poem, the content and moral tone of the piece closely approximate the requested lines. The poem has a glass of wine and a glass of water conversing on their relative merits. Beginning lines are:

> There sat two glasses filled to the brim,
> On a rich man's table, rim to rim;
> One was ruddy and red as blood,
> and one as clear as the crystal flood.

The rest of the poem consists of bragging by the glass of wine and justifications by the glass of water (Felleman, 1936).

There was a poem in German that, when translated into English, included the lines:

> **Let freedom be the purpose of restraint**
> **In the manner in which one ties up a grape vine,**
> **So that instead of creeping in the dust,**
> **It will freely twine towards the air.**

Who wrote this verse and what is the German version?

This is by Friedrich Wilhelm Weber and is titled "Dreizehnlinden" (Drenowatz, 1975) The correct wording is:

> Freiheit sei der Zweck des Zwanges
> Wie man eine rebe bindet,
> Dass sie, statt im Staub zu kriechen,
> Frei sich die Lufte windet.

There is a poem about the inmates of nursing homes, with a title such as either "Persona Non Persona" or "Non Persona Persona" Where can a copy be found?

There is a copy in the June 1973 issue of the *American Journal of Nursing.* No author is given, and the title is "Non-persona . . . Persona."

Where can I find the text of a poem that begins "Mojave Tim was a mongrel cur with a tail like a dried screw bean."

This is poem is an encomium to a man's dog. The source is not available, but copies were held at the Southern California Answering Network. The first stanza reads:

> Mojave Tim was a mongrel pup,
> With a tail like a dried screw-bean.
> His head drooped down, his ears flopped up,
> and his legs were bowed and lean.
> No artist would ever have painted him
> For the rest of the world to see,
> For he was gawky stub-nosed Tim,
> As homely as dogs can be.

Where can I find a poem about a very large cat that fights an enormous rat? The poem begins with the lines, "and that fat cat, sat on that mat, then made that rat flat!"

Operating with Law Number 4 of the Laws of Reference (coincidence is no coincidence), one "Exchange" reader sent in a poem by Tolkien (1966). It begins:

> The fat cat on the mat
> May seem to dream
> of nice mice that suffice
> For him, or cream;

Chapter 8

Artificial Nonintelligence

Once, in search of inspiration for a few leading paragraphs for a column, I went Web surfing. Incidentally, there should be a better term by now to describe one of the great time-wasting activities, truly a revenge effect of current technology. Surely it was not just by chance that the word *surfing,* describing a sport almost as silly as fox-hunting—the unspeakable in pursuit of the uneatable—was applied to this activity?

I was looking for materials on human or machine indexing of the Web. Through a lead from a listserv for freelance indexers, I found an interesting article by Leslie Walker (1996), titled "On the Web, a Catalogue of Complexity." Walker described the current competition between humans and computers to build the "biggest electronic card catalogue, the best index to the gigantic jumble that is the World Wide Web." Walker felt that while the quality of human indexing was superior to machine-generated products, eventually speed and cost demands would lead to computer-generated indexes being the only practical solution.

Of course, the computer approach has many shortcomings as well. The typical use of a search engine that generates 600,000 hits, theoretically ranked by relevance, almost always includes many completely irrelevant cites as well as links that are no longer valid. Considering that Web information is dynamic, not static, how can even computer indexes maintain any sense of order?

To continue exploring, I decided to research another popular topic—libraries offering e-mail reference services. I have done on-line searching since the early days of the *New York Times InfoBank* and feel somewhat at home online. However, even by using the sophisticated capabilities of various search engines, I retrieved many misses and few hits. Demonstrating another problem with the Web, quite a few of the sites that did look relevant returned various forms of the message, "URL not found."

The Web is clearly a marvelous resource. We all know of success stories using Web references. There are a few problems such as authenticity of sources and frequent false trails. Web searching has a fad element—when patrons feel that only electronic sources can have the best answers. However, the Web is the way of the future, and just by the nature of the beast, there is less time available to reference librarians to do the ordinary, basic kind of reference service that used to take place at a reference desk. More and more reference librarians are spending much of their time on the floor (sometimes literally) during the workday teaching patrons to use the Web. The librarians in many places also are learning to keep the workstations up and running (and spending a fair amount of time doing so). This involves not only simple tasks such as clearing off theoretically pornographic screen images but also some basic understanding of PC hardware and software, including NET and LAN applications.

I have no doubt that the Web, through its direct provision of electronic information, will alter forever how reference service, indeed information in general, is provided. We are in the early stages of a major change unlike anything since the invention of print. At the risk of sacrilege, one might compare this change to the relationship between the invention of the printing press and the Reformation. Is it really too far-fetched or even heretical to suggest that just as Reformation theologians called for a direct relationship with God without priestly intermediaries, the Web may eventually provide everyone access to full information without the intercession of a reference librarian? There is one major difference though—instead of hundreds of years, the current transition probably will be accomplished in a matter of a decade or less.

A collection from a "weird reference questions" thread that ran on LIBSUP-L, the Library Paraprofessionals Listserv in July 1997, came across my screen some time ago. As I read through the list (all purportedly real questions), I wondered how, in the Brave New Digital World of Web bots, intelligent browsers, personal information assistants, "push" technology, and artificial intelligence, these questions could ever be answered without a human interface. Odd as many of them may sound, they probably represent, albeit in a garbled way, real information needs of the questioner, and hence should never be ignored.

A list of the questions follows, with possible digital (computer) answers in italics:

> "Do you have books here?" *No.*
> "Do you have a list of all the books written in the English language?" *Yes.*
> "Do you have a list of all the books I've ever read?" *Why?*
> "I'm looking for Robert James Waller's book, 'Waltzing through Grand Rapids.'" *No match for your query. Similar titles found: The Grand Waltz; Visiting Grand Rapids; Walt's Rhapsody.*
> "Do you have that book by Rushdie: 'Satanic Nurses'?" *No.*
> "Which outlets in the library are appropriate for my hair dryer?" *None, and don't touch my plug!*
> "Can you tell me why so many famous Civil War battles were fought on National Park Sites?" *See U.S. History—1861-1865—Civil War; U.S.—National Park Service.*
> "Do you have any books with photographs of dinosaurs?" *Reserve placed on Steven Spielberg's 'Jurassic Park.'*
> "I need to find out Ibid's first name for my bibliography." *Name found in database: Ibn ben Saud.*

On the subject of garbled or really weird reference questions, years ago I remember reading a science fiction story based on what the author said was called the "Silly Season" in the news business. This came during the doldrums of summer: the time of year when there seemed to be nothing newsworthy coming across the news wires; the time when flying saucer sightings increased, rains of frogs occurred, and two-headed calves were born.

If you're familiar with the term, have you ever wondered if there might be year-round Silly Seasons in the reference rooms of libraries in this country? If we can agree that even silly questions deserve answers, then it may help to believe that a sense of humor is an important quality at a reference desk. I have a theory that successfully answering silly questions may involve some silliness on the part of the librarian. One of my personal favorites involves a question I still think of with a bit of smugness.

As received at a third-level reference service from the referring library, the question read, "The patron has an antique drinking stein with a motto around the top and he would like a translation. The patron copied the motto down, which reads *'Niso Itqui Maly Penseho.'*" It only took a few moments to answer this question and didn't involve a lot of searching through strange foreign language dictionaries, only because I think I was feeling a bit silly and said to myself, "If someone was trying to follow this around a drinking stein, who knows where they started?" With this frame of mind, *Pense* then leaped out at me, giving rise to the thought that this word was the end of the sentence and *Ho* began the phrase. Simple rearrangement then produced *Honi soit qui mal y pense,* the well-known motto of the Order of the Garter.

Chapter 9

People and Places

Searching for biographical or geographical information can be easy at the best of times and a nightmare in the worst cases—such as when the person or the place is fictional. Although there are numerous reference sources in these areas, this did not prevent the following questions in this category from ending up at "The Exchange."

*   *   *

There is an author named Judith Penderwhistle (daughter of Laszlo Reuben, a sandwich designer) listed in V. 81-84 of *Contemporary Authors*. Who was Judith Penderwhistle?

An editor at *Contemporary Authors* explained that they include a few devices to detect unauthorized or objectionable use of their material. This is one of those spurious entries.

The author Trevanian (pseudonym) has written a number of books. What is this author's real name?

A number of standard directories claim that Rodney Whitaker is Trevanian (*Contemporary Literary Criticism,* 1973; *The New York Times Book Review,* 1983; *Twentieth Century Crime and Mystery Writers,* 1980). However, a *New York Times* article (King, 1984) claims that the author of the first three Trevanian novels was James T. Hashian, a U.S. Department of Labor employee, who sold the rights to the name with the proviso that he would never reveal his authorship.

What kind of dogs did Pavlov use in his experiments?

Pavlov, unlike Western researchers who tended to use rats in their experiments, used mongrel dogs (Gray, 1979).

Who was the first black congressman elected from Illinois?

This was Oscar DePriest, who served in the seventy-first through seventy-third Congresses (1929-1935). He was a Republican from Chicago and the first black to be elected in a northern state (Christopher, 1976).

Who was the Pullman porter, the son of a slave, whose children received doctorates in medicine and philosophy?

James Julian was a railway mail clerk, born of slaves. He had six children, all of whom later graduated from DePauw University. Each of the boys later received doctorates; each of the girls held master's degrees (*Current Biography,* 1975).

Adlai Stevenson is reputed to have written some kind of defense of the rights of cats. What exactly did he say about the animals?

In a veto message to the Illinois Legislature dated April 23, 1949, Stevenson penned the following words: "I herewith return, without my approval, Senate Bill No. 93 titled, 'An Act to Provide Protection to Insectivorous Birds by Restraining Cats.'" The bill would have imposed fines on owners who permitted their cats to run at large off their premises. The full text can be found in Stevenson's papers (1973). One version includes the following reasons:

> It is in the nature of cats to do a certain amount of unescorted roaming.
>
> To escort a cat abroad on a leash is against the nature of the cat, and to permit it to venture forth for exercise unattended into a night of new dangers is against the nature of the owner.
>
> Cats perform useful service, particularly in rural areas, in combating rodents, work they necessarily perform alone and without regard for property lines.
>
> The problem of cat versus bird is as old as time. If we attempt to resolve it by legislation, who knows but what we may be called upon to take sides as well in the age-old problems of dog versus cat, bird versus bird, or even bird versus worm. (Adler, 1966)

While Paul Bunyan, the great logger, may still be a well-known name, Maine's great lobsterman, Barney Beal, is less well-known. Who was he?

Barney Beal was a giant—seven feet tall by some accounts—and a real person. His hands were so long that the palms touched the floor when he sat on an average-size chair (*Portland Sunday Telegram,* 1959). He was credited with amazing feats of strength. Once, a man offered five dollars to anyone who could lift an anchor that weighed 1,200 pounds. Barney said he would lift it, but it would squat his feet out and spoil his shoes. The man offered him a pair of shoes as well. Barney lifted the anchor. When the man would not pay, Barney carried the anchor over to the wharf and dropped it on the man's boat. He is also said to have knocked out a horse with one punch (Dorson, 1959). A picture of Barney appeared in *Downeast Magazine* (October 1978). He died in 1899, supposedly while dragging a fully loaded, fifteen-foot fishing dory over a wharf (Coffin, 1968).

George Washington Carver is said to have invented more than 118 uses for the sweet potato and more than 300 uses for the peanut. Is there a source for complete lists of these inventions?

The Tuskegee Institute (Alabama), which houses the Carver Museum, provided a list of approximately 150 uses for the peanut and around forty for the sweet potato. The list is far too extensive to quote here, but from sweet potatoes Carver made starch, tapioca, syrup, breakfast food, wood stains, flour, orange drops, yeast, and vinegar. From peanuts, he made candy, buttermilk, chili sauce, coffee, mock chicken, oleomargarine, flour, meat loaf, relish, and sausage, as well as various beverages and cosmetics (Holt, 1963; Dubois and Lipscomb, 1974).

Although the term "black Irish" may be familiar to many, its origins are somewhat murky. Is there any specific information that would positively explain the meaning of this phrase?

The *Supplement to the Oxford English Dictionary* (Oxford, 1982) is not very helpful, offering only this snippet: "Irish of Mediterranean appearance." One theory has it that Spaniards shipwrecked on the coast of Ireland after the defeat of the Spanish Armada intermarried with the Irish and produced "dark" Irish. However, as one author points out, most of the shipwrecked Spaniards were either drowned or executed, and most of the survivors were sent to back to Spain. There probably is not a lot of substance to this last explanation (Ireland, 1942).

Another explanation claims that Irish settlers in Jamaica intermarried with blacks and then migrated to the United States. Black Americans with Irish surnames have been called black Irish (Blockson, 1977). There also may be a religious association with the Protestant, or Black North, although sources for this are anecdotal, not printed.

Who are the people called the black Dutch and why are they black?

The black Dutch are "dark-complexioned of uncertain origin" (Cassidy, 1985). After that rather unhelpful explanation, Cassidy goes on to note early occurrences of the appellation. In 1854, a western explorer noted "along the center of my breast is a brown stripe like the stripe on a black Duchmans [sic] back." In another reference, Cassidy says the black Dutch are a "local type of people of Germanic extraction. They are low, not tall, small, and have black features."

Another source claims this term is used around Markham, Ontario for the Pennsylvania Dutch who settled in the area when they left Pennsylvania during the American Revolution. "Black" refers to their custom of dressing predominantly in black clothing, and "Dutch" to the fact that they emigrated to Pennsylvania from Holland, although they originally came from Germany and Switzerland.

An alternate explanation is that this refers to a group of Dutch who are natives of the southern provinces of the Netherlands, particularly North Brabant and Limberg. These people have black hair, dark skin, and blue eyes—probably because they are of Spanish-Dutch descent from the long occupation by the Spanish in the sixteenth and seventeenth centuries. Another theory holds that they were Sephardic Jews who intermarried with Dutch Protestants to escape the Inquisition (Skermetta, 1976).

Edward Leedskalnin built the Coral Castle in southern Dade County. Where can more information about this man be found?

Leedskalnin wrote a book titled *A Book in Every Home* (Leedskalnin, 1936) that contains his thoughts on love, politics, and family life. Coral Castle, in Homestead, Florida, was built between 1920 and 1940 by the Latvian immigrant. It was carved from more than 1,100 tons of solid coral bedrock. Leedskalnin used only simple chains, pulleys, and recycled auto parts to remove bedrock from the ground, shape, and hoist the rocks into precise alignments. No 600-horse-power cranes were available at the time. He worked alone, at night, and left few notes on how he created his curious collection of massive stone sculptures. A number of the pieces were signed "Ed" by the slight, ninety-five-pound man who barely topped five feet. More information is available by writing to Coral Castle, 28655 South Dixie Hwy., Homestead, FL 33030.

How did the city of Auckland (New Zealand) get its name?

The Auckland Islands were named by the discoverer, Bristow, in 1806 for the first Lord Auckland, who had been a friend of the discoverer's father. The city of Auckland's name was chosen by Governor William Hobson in 1840 after George Eden, the second Lord Auckland, who was then governor of India (Taylor, 1898). The name itself began as either Alcland, Alclet, or Aclet, from Elk-Land or Oak-Land, or as Alclyde, meaning the cliff on the Clyde. The name also has been associated with the Scandinavian *aukland,* meaning "additional land" (Ekwall, 1960). However it originated, the name ended up with a Bishop Auckland, c. 1050, and was later taken by William Eden when he was raised to the Irish peerage in 1789, becoming Baron Auckland.

While we are on the subject of naming things, what was the name of Paul Revere's horse?

Although there is not a great deal of documented evidence for this, the name commonly accepted is Brown Beauty. A genealogy of several New England families contains this report: "Samuel Larkin . . . was the owner of Brown Beauty, the mare of Paul Revere's ride, made famous by Longfellow's poem. The mare was loaned at the request of Samuel's son . . . and was never returned to her owner" (Lincoln, 1930).

What was the date of birth and birthplace of August Spies, the "Haymarket Martyr," who was executed on St. Martin's Day, November 11, 1887?

Spies was born December 10, 1855, within the ruins of the old robber's castle Landeck, upon a high mountain's peak (Landeckerberg), Germany (Foner, 1969).

Who was the "Roxy" for whom the New York theater is named?

A *New York Times* (1927) story about the opening of the Roxy Theater notes, "It is a fulfillment of the cherished ambition of Si L. Rothafel, better known as 'Roxy.'"

Is there any truth to the old story that Marie Antoinette asked why the poor could not eat cake if they had no bread?

This story was not attributed to Marie until more than half a century after her death. Fifteen years before her birth, Rousseau, in his "Confessions," pinned the yarn on an Italian noblewoman. King Louis XVIII of France in the 1820s wrote that the culprit was the wife of a predecessor, Louis XIV, who had reigned a couple of centuries before him; the only slight difference in the story is that she is supposed to have said pastry instead of cake. Also, John Peckham, a thirteenth-century Archbishop of Canterbury, tells the same story in a letter written in Latin. The French phrase is *Qu'ils mangent de la brioche* and probably meant that "they should eat the outer crust (brioche) of the bread—the stale part as opposed to the soft inside part" (*Sunday Telegraph,* 1983).

Did Queen Victoria give the German Kaiser, her cousin, Mt. Kilimanjaro as a gift?

The real reason for this land transfer was that the British recently had extended considerably their influence in Egypt and wanted German support for the move. Letting Germany have uncontested rights to the East African highlands was considered a small price to pay for diplomatic noninterference (Robinson and Gallagher, 1961).

What famous lawyer died because of overeating after he had lost an important case?

William Jennings Bryan died following a heavy meal consumed in the midst of a summer heat wave, shortly after the ending of the Scopes "Monkey Trial." However, he won the case (Darrow, 1957).

Who painted *Three Horses Frightened by a Storm*?

Gilpin Sawney did a painting called *Horses Frightened in a Thunderstorm.* This is in *Connoisseur,* May 1960, but there are more than three horses.

John Boit Morse was a twentieth-century painter supposedly of some repute, but the local library could not find any significant information on him.

Morse was a former Madison Avenue advertising executive (vice president of D'Arcy Company) who suddenly gave it all up in 1953 to become an artist. His grandfather was a drummer in the Second Massachusetts Cavalry during the Civil War and his great-grandfather was a sea captain. The family is indirectly descended from Samuel Morse, who invented the telegraph and developed Morse code (Alexander, 1986; Denison, 1982; Papineau, 1984).

Why is e. e. cummings spelled with small letters?

Supposedly this resulted from a printer's error in *Eight Harvard Poets* published in 1917. From that time on, he always signed his work "e. e. cummings" (*Lexicon Universal Encyclopedia,* n.d.). According to *Contemporary Literary Criticism* (1973), "he rarely used capital letters and until the mid-1930s preferred his own name to be written in lower case."

Why is Apollo called "Hecatebolos" and "far-darter"?

The *Larousse Encyclopedia of Mythology* (1959) explains the far-darter by allusion saying, "because the sun is murderous with its rays which strike like darts, and at the same time beneficent because of its prophylactic powers." Apollo was thought of as an archer god who shot his arrows from afar (Hecatebolos), as the god of sudden death; but also as a healer god who drove away illness.

The identity of a community subjected to exhaustive sociological analysis is often obscured when the study is published. In the introduction to his *Plainville, U. S. A.* (West, 1945), the author states:

> All place names and personal names, including my own, have been withheld or altered. This has been done out of no desire of mine for secrecy, but because every serious informant requested, and was promised, the protection of complete anonymity.

Are there ways to determine the real place names of famous studies?

In some instances, the true names of these communities have later been revealed. For example, Muncie, Indiana, was the basis for *Middletown: A Study in American Culture;* Yankee City is in fact Newburyport, Massachusetts. A patron wanted to know what the true identity of several famous "sociologically studied" cities of the twentieth century was: "Springdale," *Small Town in Mass Society: Class, Power and Religion in a Rural Community* (Vidich and Bensman, 1958); "El Cerrita," *Culture of a Contemporary Rural Community* (Leonard and Loomis, 1941); *Elmtown's Youth* (Hollingshead, 1949); and *Crestwood Heights: A Study of the Culture of Suburban Life* (Seely, Sim, and Loosley, 1956).

The librarian commented:

> I can see how this question of geography might be related to the broader question of "disguised" cities in literature generally: from Batman's Gotham City to Thomas Wolfe and Altamont, North Carolina. In the case of fiction, literary license perhaps allows speculation about the locations that inspired writers. But in the instance of case studies, where individuals and towns have had their souls laid bare, should identities be revealed? On the other hand, if the information is available, isn't it fair game for librarians and their patrons? (Albertson, 1980)

Although strictly speaking there was no further answer to the patron's question, this one is included because of the information about Middletown and Yankee City.

Chapter 10

Universal Access—Free and Open Access—It Depends

It depends on where you live. The values of universal access are much older than the present legislative attempts. The whole public library movement, in one sense, was based on providing everyone with access to information and education, regardless of accidents of geographic location. The Carnegie philanthropic projects aided this idea. However, I have to wonder how much progress we really have made toward the ideal of every citizen of this country having equal access to information regardless of where they live or where they may travel. Yes, the percentage of public libraries theoretically providing Web access has been growing. However, simply providing a workstation is only one small step toward providing universal access. A big hurdle may have to be overcome—staff and community attitudes. This was borne out by an experience with library service in the Midwest.

On a vacation to visit family in Iowa, I needed to check something on the Web. I stopped at the nearest local library. There was one workstation devoted to the Internet, and although it was not in use when I was there, this terminal was available *only* to local library cardholders. The staff seemed to know very little about Internet access or such things as a telecommunications discount for universal access—or to care. I went on to the library in a neighboring city. This second location was just a short drive away, less than five miles. The two cities seem to consider themselves "sister cities" and publish a joint Chamber of Commerce Visitors Guide but share little in common in their libraries' approach to access to worldwide information.

At the second library I found a completely different picture. I found a staff excited about the Internet and Web opportunities. I found five graphics Web workstations and several text-based Internet PCs. I also found openness to experimentation and a willingness to provide access to the world of information to anyone who came in the door—regardless of where someone paid property taxes.

Granted, the library in the first city is smaller, with per capita support of approximately $34. The second city has per capita support of about $44. However, per capita support should not affect the way that a library staff perceives access to information.

Another disturbing trend that seems to be surfacing in some libraries is the tendency to block off or otherwise limit access from some public terminals to the Internet. Ostensibly this is done to preserve access to "The Library Catalog." However, this has to be seen for exactly what it is—an attempt by library staff to control access to information. If not an issue of control, it may be, as some librarians privately note, to keep out some classes of troublesome users—such as teenagers. In other situations, librarians, again ostensibly with good motives, have set up situations where one PC is for the Internet, another PC is for the catalog, the next PC is for word processing, etc.

Librarians who institute these control measures are missing the point completely. Instead of continuing the grand tradition of "The People's University" from the early days of public librarianship in the United States, these libraries are harking back, albeit unknowingly, to the medieval concept of a library where access was controlled by the monks. Everyone in the library business needs to recognize that "The Library Catalog" has become only one node in the world of online information. Preselecting what information users can access on what machine comes dangerously close to censorship. It is as if the library has opened a candy store and then said, "You can only pick one piece of candy a day and today it will have to be from the blue tin."

Chapter 11

Words and Phrases

What is the origin of the bowling term, "on the Brooklyn side"?

New Yorkers facing south in old-time bowling alleys called a strike on the right side of the headpin a "Jersey" hit because New Jersey was on their right. A strike on the left side, then, was on the "Brooklyn" side.

Two words in the English language that end in "gry" are "angry" and "hungry." What is a third word ending in "gry"?

Many words, most rather esoteric, end in "gry," as a search of the *Oxford English Dictionary on CD-ROM* using left-hand truncation establishes. Some examples are: aggry, pigry, iggry, meagry, mawgry, nangry, podagry, puggry, and skugry.

There is an alternate form of this riddle. It must be spoken and heard; it does not work if written down. As this version goes, the statement is, "There are at least three words in the English language that end in *g* or *y*. One of them is hungry and another is angry. There is a third word, a short one, which you probably say everyday. If you are listening carefully to everything I say, you just heard me say it three times. What is it? The answer is 'say' which ends in *y*."

There are several other forms of this riddle. In one, the third and fourth line read, "there are only three words in the English language. What is the third word?" (Answer: "language," the third word in "the English language.") There is a fascinating discussion of the riddle at <http://www.worldwidewords.org>.

What words end in the suffix *"-dous"* besides tremendous, stupendous, horrendous, hazardous, and jeopardous?

Those are the most common, but there are many more such words. An abbreviated list includes tongue-twisting examples such as:

palladous, vanadous, tardigradous, iodous, octopodous, rhizopodous, nonhazardous, timidous, amphipodous, pygopodous, brachiopodous (Lehnert, 1971). *The Normal and Reverse English Word List* has 130 listings of "dous" words.

Here is one last "word ending" question: Besides cushion and fashion, what other words end in shion?

Two more words are hushion (a stocking without a foot) and pin-cushion.

What is prad-prigging?

Prad-prigging was horse stealing. A repentant (but still hanged) thief named John Poulter described this and many other crimes in an attempt to avoid the noose (Poulter, 1779). In *The Second Part of Conny-Catching* (Greene, 1966), there is a "pleasant storie of a horse-stealer" wherein the priggar "went to heauen on a string and many of his faculty had don before." An interesting essay on the profession can be found in a section on "The Prigging Law," in *The Belman of London, Bringing to Light the Most Notorius Villanies that Are Now Practised in the Kingdome* (Dekker, 1973).

What is meant by the reference to "King John's Apples" in Franklin's story "The Whistle"?

Several references, including the *Oxford English Dictionary*, suggest this refers to apples that keep for a long time but become very withered. Another writer notes that King John (1161?-1216) of England was supposedly poisoned by a monk who gave him a bad apple.

There is a reference to some things called Irish Treasurer's Wagons in the papers of James Madison. What were these wagons?

At one point, William Wood minted some inferior copper coins for Ireland, which Jonathan Swift noted could be driven safely through the country since a highwayman would scorn to touch them. The allusion then attached itself to wagons from the Treasury (Davis, 1965; Mays, 1967).

On an exam for bartender, the following question was posed: "What is a Carl Spangler?" Is this a drink?

The best response was that the person asking the question misheard and really was referring to Bill Murray's character, Carl Spackler, in the film *Caddyshack.*

Where did the phrase "dance with the devil in the pale moonlight" come from? Supposedly it was used in the movie *Batman* by Jack Nicholson, playing the Joker.

This allusion may have come from John Masefield's poem "Captain Stratton's Fancy," which includes this stanza:

> Oh, some are fond of red wine and some are fond of white,
> and some are all for dancing by the pale moonlight,
> But rum alone's the tipple and the heart's delight
> of the old, bold mate of Henry Morgan.

Does the name "Teddy" for an envelope chemise come from the association of Teddy Roosevelt with the teddy bear?

A Dictionary of Slang and Unconventional English (Partridge, 1984) does say that the combination of camisole and loose panties called a teddy during the period 1920-1940 was named after Teddy Roosevelt. What is lacking is any explanation about how a dainty lady's garment came to be associated with the Rough Rider's first name, but it does raise some interesting, if salacious, thoughts.

To muddy the waters a bit, the *Oxford English Dictionary* attributes the name to "a real or fancied resemblance in general shape (or shapelessness) to the teddy-bear." Not only is this definition wishy-washy, but you have to wonder where the editors of the *OED* were cloistered.

What is the origin and meaning of the phrase "alarums and excursions"?

In early modern English drama, *alarums* and *excursions* was a stage direction referring to representative fragments of sounds from a military action. *Alarum* is a "call to arms, summons." *Excursion* is used "to indicate that groups of soldiers run across the stage; usually to stimulate a battle" (Martin and Harrier, 1971; Random House, 1996).

What is the origin of the phrase "Black Is Beautiful"?

One possible source might be the Song of Solomon (1:5), which reads, "I am black but beautiful, O ye daughters of Jerusalem." Also, Langston Hughes wrote in *The Negro Artist and the Racial Moun-*

tain, "Why should I want to be white? I am a Negro—and beautiful" (*The Harlem Renaissance,* 2001).

Where did the nickname "Big Apple" for New York come from?

The name was originally used in the 1920s and 1930s by people in the sports and entertainment world—a way of saying, "I've made it to the big time, I'm playing in New York—the Big Apple." In other words, there are many apples on the tree, but there is only one Big Apple. Various samples of the phrase are:

- Why should she stay in the Apple over a July weekend?
- As soon as we hit the Big Apple, we'll ditch the buggy.
- The big town, the main stem, Harlem.

Possibly the phrase was a transliteration of an older Mexicom idiom, *Manzane principale* for the main square of a town (Gold, 1975). A dance called the Big Apple appeared about 1935 in New York; however, it is believed to have originated at the Big Apple Club in Columbia, South Carolina (Raffe, 1964).

Is there a word for someone who collects knives?

The National Knife Collectors Association (NKCA) proposed "machairologist" and "machairology", based on the Greek word for knife. Every field has its own hot controversy, and apparently The American Blade Collectors objected to the harsh sound of this name and suggested "coutelics" and "coutelist" (from an old French word for cutlery) instead (Parker, 1984). At the end of the cited note, the then vice-president of the NKCA is quoted as saying, "I don't know what's wrong with calling a knife collector a 'knife collector.'"

What is the name for someone who collects bottles?

A collector of beer bottles is known as a labeorphilist, but there does not seem to be a more general term for all bottle collecting (Urdang, 1986).

What is the origin of the Mardi Gras term "krewe"?

This is a term with Old English flavor, first used by the Krewe of Comus in New Orleans in 1857 to name a Carnival organization.

What is the translation of the Indian name *Gitchee Gumee?*

Although this question was not received by "The Exchange," it well could have been. I include it to give an example of serendipity in reference work. Another librarian had verified that this was from Longfellow's *Song of Hiawatha*. I remembered using a section in the *Handbook of American Indians North of Mexico* (Hodge, 1979) that provided a glossary of Indian names and words. Looking in this book under Gitchee I found this entry: "Gittci's—Kitzeesh." To pursue this lead I started to flip over to the K's, and the book, which is quite thick, first fell open on page 705 where the running head read "Kitaix—Kitchigami."

With the guidance of the Fourth Commandment of Reference Work (see Chapter 2), "Coincidence is no coincidence," my eye immediately dropped to the half-column entry on Kitchigami. According to this, the word meant "great water" from *kitchi* (great) and *gami* (water), the Chippewa name for Lake Superior. The Kitchigami were a tribe living in central or southwest Wisconsin in 1669-1670 and related to the Kickapoo and Mascoutens.

Although Hiawatha was an Iroquois chief who lived far from Lake Superior, Longfellow, who got many of his ideas about Indian life from the ethnologist Henry Rowe Schoolcraft, repeated a mistake by Schoolcraft. Schoolcraft confused the Iroquois Hiawatha with the Chippewa Manabozho, which led Longfellow to set the *Song of Hiawatha* on the shores of Lake Superior instead of in central New York (Benét, 1987).

Why do they call a flower holder a "frog"?

Presumably the word comes from the French *fourche* (fork). *Fourche* derives from *fourchette* (fork, frame, branchwood, etc.). Some French dictionaries translate frog as *fourchette*.

What is the distinction between an undercroft and a crypt?

Most sources define the two terms as synonymous, with "crypt" more specifically referring to a place of burial. *The English Mediaeval Parish Church* states that "the line of development of the crypt was from the tomb under the altar to the undercroft of the sanctuary. . . . In some instances the steep slope of the ground at the east end of a church necessitated the construction of an undercroft or crypt on which to rear the chancel" (Cook, 1954). *English Abbeys* (Braun,

1971) notes that "the most common feature encountered in the two-storied domestic architecture of the abbeys is the vaulted undercroft, carrying the main floor over, and always having a row of pillars down its center." Some sources that discuss the development of the crypt and its purpose are: *The Heritage of the Cathedral* (Prentice, 1934), *The Evolution of Church Building* (Bowyer, 1977), and *Cathedral Architecture* (Braun, 1972).

What do you call a kaleidoscope that has no moving parts?

In other words, when is a kaleidoscope not a kaleidoscope? When it is a *teleidoscope* (*Smithsonian Catalogue,* 1988).

Where did the phrase (and the language) "Pig Latin" originate?

There are several types of Pig Latin. One is also referred to as "Dog Latin." This form has been around for decades before World War I, probably at least from the mid-eighteenth century (Morris and Morris, 1977). This latter consists of decapitated English words, the initial letters transposed to the rear, plus "ay"; as "Ohnay-jay ust-may o-gay ome-hay" for "John must go home" (Funk, 1958). Some think the name came from a sound resembling the grunting of hogs. On the other hand, Dog or Pig Latin can also be pretend Latin, as in a kitchen is "camera necessaria pro usus cookare; cum saucepannis, stew-pannis, scullero, dressero, coalholo stovis, smoak-jacko; pro roast-andum boilandrum fryandum et plum-pudding mixandum" (Brewer, 1970).

What is "pure quill"?

Pure quill is a piece of cinnamon or cinchona bark curled up in the form of a tube (*Oxford English Dictionary Supplement,* 1982). The term can be applied to other materials, for example in drug use: "Quill: folded matchbook cover in which a narcotic is held and smoked or sniffed" (Major, 1970).

Where did the saying "He's a born gosling" come from?

Charles Funk explained:

> American pronunciation is such that, to some speakers, "gone" becomes "gawn," and to some, "born" becomes "bawn"—and the two could become confused if the listener wasn't quite paying full attention. . . . A "gone gosling" is identical to a "dead

duck." Both terms are given in the new Supplement (A-G) of OED . . . under "gone" and "dead," respectively—in fact, the "gone gosling" is the leading term under "gone" whereas a bit of a search is required to find the "dead duck." (Funk, 1975)

What is *Hunan Hand?*

This medical condition (contact dermatitis associated with capsaicin, especially chili peppers) is described in a book by Moskow (1987). The work is a compendium of correspondence originally appearing in the *New England Journal of Medicine* describing unusual reasons for visiting a doctor or emergency room. A brief list of syndromes includes:

> Back-pocket sciatica, caused by carrying thick wallets or golf balls in the hip pocket; Lawn-mower arm, from too strenuous use of a starter cord; Reflex horn syndrome, drivers who depress their horns several milliseconds after a red light turns green; and cinematic neurosis, induced by such movies as *Jaws*.

A second book, *Syndromes for the Layperson* (Dixon, 1988) includes descriptions not only of bona fide medical syndromes but also conditions resulting from modern living such as anniversary reaction, answering machine hang-up, and dog walker's elbow.

A patron thought that Earl Warren may have originated the legal term "dead hand of the past." Is this the case?

"Dead hand" comes from the legal concept of mortmain, which goes back at least as far as the thirteenth century, according to *The Oxford Dictionary of the English Language* (OED, 1989). When people spoke of a "dead hand," they were referring to the practice of someone tying up their property after their death via a trust or a will. The "dead hand" was figuratively reaching out of the grave and affecting living people. It could also refer to impersonal ownership, such as when the Church took over lands. The specific phrase appeared in a law case from 1912, with this sentence, "Progress and betterment should not be denied . . . by the dead hand of the past." Earl Warren was still in law school at that time.

What is the origin of the toast "to absent friends"?

Use of the phrase "absent brethren" can be found in Masonic rituals dating back to World War I. Prior to this, "to all brethren wheresoever dispersed" was in general use by 1756. The toast to absent friends is said to have attained a measure of popularity during the Napoleonic wars. It was adopted into the toast lists of most English lodges during World War I (*Ars Quatuor Coronatorum*, 1969).

Jacques Cartier's description of his voyage to the Iles de la Madeleine (Eastern Canada) in 1534 refers to some birds: *des margaux, des apponatz, des godez.* The names did not appear in any available French dictionaries or bird books, so the reference librarian wrote to "The Exchange" for help.

Several readers supplied translations. *Margaux* were gannets, *apponatz* were the great auks, and *godez* were razor-billed auks (Biggar, 1924). There was a suggestion that *margaux* was a misspelling of "margots," or "magpie," but this was ruled highly unlikely because the magpie is not found in Eastern Canada except as a rare escaped cage bird.

How did the term "bulldog edition" of a newspaper originate?

"In the 1890s several New York City newspapers brought out early morning editions that came to be called *bulldog editions,* possibly because the newspapers 'fought like bulldogs' among themselves in their circulation wars" (Hendrickson, 1987; Hoyt, 1940).

Supposedly during the days of slavery in the South, medical professionals claimed that a mental condition caused slaves to try to run away—never mind that the physical condition of slavery could have produced a corresponding mental desire to be free! What was this supposed mental condition called?

It is true that some Southern doctors believed that blacks were susceptible to unique physical and mental disorders. A Louisiana physician, Dr. Samuel W. Cartwright, recorded that slaves were prone to mental disorders that he labeled *Dysaethesia Ethiopica* and *Drapetomania.* "The slave suffering from *Dyaesthesia Ethiopica* . . . broke toes, damaged crops, and endangered livestock." The doctor noted that the first symptom of *Drapetomania* was a dissatisfied attitude, which, if unchecked, caused the slave to run away (Bell, 1980). The word *drapetomania* was derived from the Greek *drapetos,* or runaway slave, and *mania,* mad or crazy (Breeden, 1980).

Different explanations, ranging from Edgar Bergen's dummy Mortimer Snerd to "knurd" (drunk spelled backward) to "gnerd" (an acronym for Gross, Nervous, Evasive, Repulsive, and Disgusting) exist for the derivation of the word *"nerd"* (Dvorak, 1987). What was the real origin of this term?

Back in 1950 Dr. Seuss wrote a book titled *If I Ran the Zoo* (Geisel, 1950). In it, he drew (and named) a character called a nerd. Seuss says he never heard the word before he drew that character (Dvorak, 1987).

Is there a word for sentences such as "The quick brown fox jumped over the lazy dog's back" that use all twenty-six letters of the alphabet?

The word is "pangram." Pangrammatic verses are "far older than the thirteenth century" (OED, 1989). Some other examples:

- Pack my box with five dozen liquor jugs.
- Waltz, nymph, for quick jigs vex Bud.
- The five boxing wizards jump quickly. (Dickson, 1982)

According to the *Guinness Book of World Records* (1988), the shortest pangram is "Veldt jynx grimps waqf zho buck." The sentence is used to describe the situation in which a wryneck woodpecker from the grasslands of Africa climbs up the side of a male bovid that is grazing on sacred Muslim-owned land.

What is the origin of the sentence used for typing practice since the early days of the typewriter: "Now is the time for all good men to come to the aid of their party"?

Charles E. Weller is supposed to have used this sentence to test the first practical typewriter in 1867. However, Weller did not claim credit for this in his book *The Early History of the Typewriter* (Weller, 1918). *Respectfully Quoted* (Platt, 1993) says the author is unknown.

It is also debatable whether the machine used in 1867 could be called the first typewriter, since other inventions for doing the same that predated it. Whether or not the sentence began with the first practical typewriter is probably of less interest than the next use of the phrase. In 1868 the slogan was used in Ulysses S. Grant's presidential campaign.

What is the term for words that have definitions that are the same and opposite? For example, *"fast"* can mean hold firmly in one place, as in "the pegs held the tent fast," and move rapidly from place to place, as in "she ran fast."

These words are called contranyms or, more popularly, Janus-faced words (Lederer, 1989). Another example is "clip"—you can clip coupons from a newspaper, or you can clip coupons to a newspaper. Or, "The moon is *out* [visible] tonight," and "the lights in the house are *out* [not visible] tonight."

What is the term for the @ (at) sign?

This is called a commercial A (Robinson, 1972; Updike, 1927).

What is the name of the king who, rather than modify his bed, cut off the feet of visitors too long to fit or stretched the legs of those with physiques too short?

This question generated possibly the most answers ever received by "The Exchange." The king was Procrustes and one source for the legend is MacCulloch (1932).

Staying on the classics, what is the epigram that sums up the Epicurean philosophy?

Twelve words, inscribed in a cloister in Lycia by Diogenes of Oenoana, give a concise summation of Epicurean philosophy (Harvey, 1937): "Nothing to fear in God. Nothing to fear in Death. Good can be attained. Evil can be endured."

From the classics to the not-so-classics, "The Exchange" covered all genres. One puzzler had to do with the meaning of a "Cheltenham Tragedy."

Although there was no clear, documented answer for this, one reader surmised that the phrase was the equivalent of a "tempest in a teapot," deriving from turgid and overacted tragedies performed during the 1880s for the enjoyment of people who visited various spas to take Cheltenham salts and waters (Woudenberg, 1980).

From **teapot tempest**, it seems natural to bring up a tall tale that led to the appellation "Scott's coon." Ely S. Parker, Commissioner of Indian Affairs during Ulysses S. Grant's administration, in speeches referring to Lee's surrender, used these phrases: "Like Scott's coon, I say, 'Don't shoot'" and "He became at once like the coon with the redoubtable Scott, willing to come down."

An anecdote in *Captain Frederick Marryat's Diary in America* (Zanger, 1954) tells the story of Captain Martin Scott, who was a remarkable shot. He went out one morning and, spying a raccoon on the upper branches of a tree, brought his rifle up to his shoulder. The raccoon asked him if his name was Captain Martin Scott. When Scott said yes, the raccoon said, "I might as well come down, for I'm a gone coon." This was the origin of the expression "gone coon."

Where did the "submarine sandwich" originate and why the name?

The idea of a very long sandwich, filled with meat, cheese, lettuce, and tomato (plus whatever the imagination of the cook could add) goes back in this country at least to the nineteenth century. At that time, New Orleans tourists reported on sandwiches called poor boys. Besides meat, they included vegetables and even appetizers. Some of these sandwiches were built with the appetizer at one end, meat in the middle, and cheese or something sweet at the end, so one could eat one's way through a full-course meal (Flexner, 1982).

A sandwich called the submarine sandwich was introduced to the world by an Italian grocer in New London, Connecticut, during World War II. His name was Benedetto Capaldo. Capaldo is pictured holding a huge sandwich in *The Best of the Old Farmer's Almanac* (Hale, 1991). Capaldo sold the sandwiches to sailors at the Groton-New London submarine base. This accounts for Groton's claim that it is the submarine capital of the world.

This was not the first appearance of the word "submarine" connected with a sandwich. An earlier use in 1916 is noted, quoting a waiter, "Two submarines and a mug of murk—no cow" (OED, 1989). Moreover, a letter published in William Safire's (1980) *On Language* contends that the name sub or even submarine was never used for sandwiches anywhere near the London/New Groton area. The sandwiches in this area were always called grinders. Other names for this kind of sandwich are: spuky, wedge, hoagy (or hoagie), poor boy, hero, and Cuban.

During World War I, a popular phrase was "Whizbang Willie." What was the origin of this term?

This could be connected to the magazine *Captain Billy's Whiz Bang* referred to in *The Music Man,* where "telling jokes from *Captain Billy's Whiz Bang*" was seen as a sign of corruption. The magazine was published from 1919 through the 1920s (Moore, 1995).

There is a series of phrases that serve as tests of memory, beginning: "one hen, two ducks, three squawking geese, four limerick oysters, five corpulent corpuscles." The librarian hoped one "Exchange" reader would remember these phrases. Where can the full text be found?

Try to remember this now!

> One hen, two ducks, three squawking geese, four limerick oysters, five corpulent porpoises, six pairs of Don El Verzo's tweezers, seven thousand Macedonians in full battle array, eight brass monkeys from the ancient, sacred crypts of Egypt, nine apathetic, sympathetic, diabetic old men on roller skates with a marked propensity for procrastination and sloth, ten lyrical, spherical, diabolical denizens of the deep who stall around the corner of the quo of the quay of the quivy, all at the same time. (Larson, 1992; Bunner, 1992)

The word *wecca* appeared in this Christmas card quote: "Our Christmas ritual is but a momentary freezing of time with its smells of fun and fresh wecca." What is *wecca*?

In the context given, there is some logic for assuming that the "w" in wecca resulted from a typesetter's error in inverting the "m" in mecca balsam. Mecca balsam is an oleoresin obtained from balm of Gilead (balsam fir), a tree commonly used as a Christmas tree (Pate, 1988).

What is a word for attributing animal characteristics to inanimate objects?

General dictionary sources suggest "animalize" or "zoomorphism".

What is the origin of the expression "the third place"?

A "third place" is neither a workplace nor a homeplace, but a place where one can find pleasant companions, stimulating conversation, inspiration, etc. This is how coffeehouses in late sixteenth- and early seventeenth-century London were described, as by Addison and Steele. Unfortunately, no more specific reference arrived at "The Exchange."

Who coined the word "Yuppie"?

Presumably it stands for Young Urban Professional, but who actually said it first remains a mystery, at least as far as "The Exchange" is concerned.

Chapter 12

Right or Wrong—What's the Question?

One reader asked if there was a term for answering a question with a question. What a perfect question from a reference librarian! After all, don't we frequently do just this? Of course, we call it "the reference interview" or "negotiating the question." I sometimes wonder how patrons feel when they ask what they think is a very simple question, only to have the librarian come back with another question. Patrons probably don't realize that the librarian was trained to assume patrons don't know what they really want.

In response to my comment about this issue of assuming the patron is not asking the real question, James Rettig, from the Earl Gregg Swem Library, College of William and Mary in Virginia, wrote a lengthy and thoughtful response (Rettig, 1991). I agreed with most of what he said in principle but differed on several points in practice. The difference of opinion, it seems to me, may point to what is beginning to emerge as an issue of what reference librarianship will be like in the coming decades. A good look into one possible future can be found in "When We Get the Libraries We Want, Will We Want the Libraries We Get?" (Seiler and Suprenant, 1991).

Rettig began by calling attention to my statement, "The patron probably doesn't realize that librarians are trained to assume the patron doesn't really know what he/she really wants." He goes on to say:

> I hope none of us has been trained to assume the patron doesn't know what he/she really wants! The reason reference librarians should negotiate even seemingly self-explanatory questions such as "Where are the encyclopedias?" is that we are engaged in interpersonal communication, a fragile process always fraught with peril and subject to failure if one party misunderstands the other. . . . To use an analogy—I think when a client comes to a professional, he or she expects that professional to apply that

profession's body of knowledge to solve a problem. I don't
think clients expect to tell the professional what specific strategy to follow to solve the problem. For example, would a patient
reasonably go to a doctor's office and demand a prescription for
a particular drug and expect to receive that drug without a doctor's first asking some questions and conducting an examination? No. We expect a physician to apply his or her knowledge
of medicine to a patient's problem and then, based on that
knowledge and the results of the examination, to prescribe a
course of treatment. Why should it be any different at the reference desk?

In responding to Rettig, I first acknowledged that I have a tendency
to overstate the case—paint with broad strokes—to get people to
think about a point. However, I still perceive several differences in
our approach. For one, I prefer a definition of "professional" from a
behavioral viewpoint rather than a sociological one. To me, "professional" can describe a continuum of services instead of a single
"professional" catalog of characteristics that one finds in the "professional" literature of librarianship where writers lay out the characteristics of a profession.

Consequently, I have never bought the analogy relating librarians
to doctors. Because, no matter how important access to information
is, librarianship is almost never (except possibly for some cases in
medical reference) a life-or-death profession. It really would be
stretching the imagination to think that someone might die because a
book was miscataloged or a reference question answered incorrectly.
With some stretch of the imagination, you can postulate a case in
which a patron calls a public library reference desk for help because
he or she has taken some poison and the librarian provides the wrong
answer. Maybe this has even happened, although I suspect such a
case would have received national attention. If librarianship were
truly a life-or-death profession in the same way as medicine, then we
would all be covered by malpractice insurance. This does not mean
that I do not find reference librarianship a noble and important calling—after all, it has been my profession for thirty years!

We may see the profession from the different perspectives of working in an academic library operating at a slower pace and in many
busy public libraries that seem chronically understaffed. At an average rate of a different question every three minutes at a busy public li-

brary reference desk, an extended dialog to negotiate every question with every patron is simply not possible. Despite a philosophical commitment to gaining a full understanding of every patron's need, practicality forces many public library reference librarians to operate on the triage principle. If someone asks "where is the Readers' Guide?" they may be directed to the table with this index—hopefully with a quick reminder to "come back if you don't find what you need." This last comment can make or break a reference interaction. It is called follow-up. Some authorities recommend simply asking, "Does that completely answer your question?" which is probably impractical in many library situations. At the very least, once should always reassure the patron that returning to the desk for more information if needed is desirable.

Regarding the initial point of contention, I remember library school professors hammering the point that "patrons never ask their real question." I should have phrased my original comment this way, instead of saying we were trained to assume patrons do not know what they want.

The larger point, however, lies in the implications of the coming digitizing of information described by Seiler and Suprenant (1991). Writers have been forecasting the end of the library and the book for so many years that many readers find it difficult to take another such article seriously. However, it now seems quite possible that electronic libraries and direct patron access to information (both of which may well bypass the library and librarians as we know them) will become reality. If this is indeed the future—and it certainly seems we are headed this way—the type of reference librarianship Rettig advocates (and the type I wish we had time to practice) probably will someday be referred to as twentieth-century reference librarianship in the same way we think about the quiet, stately, and somewhat quaint practice of librarianship in the nineteenth century.

For now, all we can do is try to improve services in two major areas: (1) facilitating the patron's access to all information by whatever means necessary; and (2) reducing the communication barriers that exist between a patron's need to know and the librarian's understanding of that need.

These communication barriers account for, at least in part, the recurring concern over a perceived lack of accuracy in answering questions—the so-called "half-right" reference problem. The reference literature of librarianship includes a number of studies relating to this problem. These articles usually refer to studies purporting to show that only half of reference questions asked are answered correctly. Other studies have suggested that the set of test questions used to "prove" this dismal rate represent a very small fraction of the total questions asked at a reference desk. I do not know which side is correct, but I think the case is still open. Certainly there is nothing wrong with trying to improve information services—we all make mistakes at times.

A good example of human fallacy in reference was the question about the origin of the word "nerd". John Dvorak (1987), in his column in *PC Magazine,* noted that many librarians had sent him the same page from the *Second Barnhart Dictionary of New English* (Barnhart, Steinmetz, and Barnhart, 1980), giving a mid-1960s origin (from the 1940s surfer's term "nert"). Dvorak had other colorful explanations from readers such as the acronym "Neurotic Engineers in R & D," all dating from the early 1960s. However, one person found "nerd" in a book published in 1950—Dr. Seuss' *If I Ran the Zoo* (and the character even looks like a nerd) (Geisel, 1950). Obviously at least some librarians had missed the answer to this question.

We do miss answers. All of us. I reviewed a book on factors influencing the likelihood of reference librarians finding the correct answer. This book cited a number of the studies on reference inaccuracy—a depressingly low percentage of correct answers seem to emerge from every study of reference effectiveness, whether the study was obtrusive or unobtrusive. As a reference manager I always viewed these studies with a mixture of pity (for those poor other libraries) and complacency (knowing it couldn't be true in my library).

The nerd answer, though, really gave me pause. I must admit, if I had been working on the reference desk when I got that question, I would probably have turned up the Barnhart dictionary answer and given it to the patron. If I were doing output measures or otherwise tracking reference answers, I would have marked it as a question answered correctly. However, if this question was on an unobtrusive study, I suppose it would have been counted as an incorrect answer. Now, if serendipity were operating, I would have just read *If I Ran the Zoo* to my daughter the night before getting the question and would have come up with the right answer. Unfortunately, my daughter and Dr. Seuss were at least twelve years apart at the time of this question, so there probably would have been no hope of getting it right (unless I was a children's librarian!).

My first conclusion to these ruminations was, "It's about time we did an unobtrusive study at our library!" Then I moved into a philosophical mood (especially since I was short on answers to questions for the column that month). Perhaps we should ask ourselves, "What is a right answer?" It seems to me there is a measure of absolutism in those unobtrusive studies. There have been instances in "The Exchange" where half a dozen printed sources later proved incorrect. Many librarians probably thought the nerd question had been answered correctly.

The typical unobtrusive study picks twenty to thirty questions to test accuracy. All the questions are well tested and presumably could be answered correctly. If only 50 percent are answered "correctly," the researcher concludes that the library has a low accuracy rate. However, a typical public library in a midsize city may handle over 7,000 reference (not including directional) transactions a month. This works out to about twenty-three per hour, or just under three minutes per question. Because of a limited budget, these questions often are answered by librarians who work almost the entire day on the reference desk. If I picked any thirty of those 7,000 questions and found half answered incorrectly, could I conclude that those librarians were doing a poor job of answering questions? Or should I conclude, heretically, that imperfection is inherent in the reference business, particularly in a world full of nerdy (not stupid, just nerdy) questions, understaffing, and long, stressful hours behind a desk holding oneself out as the source of information about everything under the sun?

I said I was philosophical—and here comes the philosophy. I conclude that reference librarianship is an existential art. The reference librarian exists as a nexus between Answers, floating around in the cosmos that is our "library resource," and Questions that are at best frequently only half-understood and many times not answered immediately to the satisfaction of the patron. I am willing to trust many years of observation more than thirty unobtrusive questions. Staff I have worked with, and in a number of cases trained, usually do a darn good job of matching the right answer to the right question. Sometimes this happens serendipitously. Sometimes the patron who asks the question is not the one who eventually gets the answer. But perhaps there is some rightness to the world if you believe that each bit of knowledge passed on will eventually come to rest with someone who needs that knowledge—just as someone someday will find the correct explanation of nerd. It also helps to realize that, in Joe E. Brown's famous concluding line in the film *Some Like It Hot,* "Nobody's perfect."

No matter what percentage of questions we really answer correctly, there may be a more important point that we are missing, particularly concerning the plunge into new technological ways of providing information. Maybe librarians sometimes feel pressure to meet artificial expectations, particularly those introduced by new technology, especially expectations of our profession rather than those of our patrons.

I am not suggesting that we should not have high expectations, but sometimes I think we may take ourselves too seriously in our drive to be "professionals." Sometimes the patron really does want to know where the encyclopedias are. This person may resent a five-minute "reference interview." It would not hurt to keep in mind that using an RIM (response initiation mechanism) is not always necessary. An RIM, by the way, is what the field of discourse analysis calls answering a question with a question. For example: Q: "What time did you come in?" A: "Do I have to answer that?" This is RIM—questioning the authority of the questioner, as opposed to simply answering the question by saying, "nine o'clock." It is also an integral part of the "reference interview."

This reference interview and the corresponding skills to put what is learned in the interview to use is not a qualification easily found in librarians. During at least fifteen years of interviewing librarians for reference jobs, I have often wished there were one question that would single out the stars. By stars I mean the reference librarians who almost always do an excellent reference interview, head right for the correct source, and follow up with the user. I know these people exist, and I have been fortunate to have worked with a number of them. However, I have also seen reference librarians who, depending on a wide variety of internal and external factors, may or may not do a decent interview. After looking in half a dozen sources, this kind of librarian may find a satisfactory answer or may give up, sometimes rationalizing that the press of business prevents full service. But the stars seem able to handle a faster pace of questions than their colleagues and rarely become flustered or stressed out.

The really good reference librarians do not have ego problems that prevent them from seeking advice from co-workers or even from a patron. They do not seem to be concerned that they may look less than completely knowledgeable in front of a patron. These staff members are eager to use new ways to provide information—and they react to new technology with unabashed interest and a willingness to experiment. Unfortunately, observations in different libraries around the country and conversations at conventions indicate to me that our profession still may include its share of technophobes—the twentieth-century version of Luddites—librarians who are determined not to let technology touch them.

These are the staff members who refuse to use new products, often using the rationalization that they have not received adequate training. Even in the face of clear evidence that a significant number of users (often the young) may be perfectly comfortable using new ways to access information, this kind of librarian resists the implementation of new technology. Ironically, the same technophobic librarians usually will not hesitate to jump in with a new print reference source and use it without committing to memory every feature. I have finally come to believe that one basic characteristic good reference librarians share is a sense of curiosity and wonder—and a willingness to jump in and experiment with new tools.

On the subject of those new tools and, more specifically, some old ones, a perennial question is whether (and what) to weed from the reference collection. This has become more important as increasing space is given to hardware at the expense of printed tools. I suspect reference librarians are inveterate hoarders.

It is possible to approach weeding the circulating collection with an enlightened attitude and really get rid of the things that no one is reading, but how do you throw away a reference book, particularly when no new edition has been published? Probably every reference collection has books that have not been touched in years. When I look at an old favorite, I wonder—if it is discarded, is Murphy's Law going to operate and someone approach the desk a week later with a question only that discarded book could answer?

Certainly reference books with outdated information should be discarded. Or should they? A complete set of the *World Almanac* is a priceless reference treasure. I have seen reference librarians discard an old edition of *Granger's* when a newer one came—not realizing, I suppose, that each *Granger's* is unique and contains some poems that other editions do not. Obviously our reference shelves aren't infinitely expandable—so something has to go. With all the bibliographies floating around, all the scholarly studies being done by faculty at library schools, and all the term paper assignments given to library science students, wouldn't it be nice to see something like "The 100 Absolutely Useless Reference Books Which Everyone Could Safely Discard"?

The source for an answer to what might have seemed like a trivial question came from an old reference book that might have been discarded if overaggressive reference weeding had been practiced. This particular question also is a good illustration of the psychic benefits that can accrue as a result of dedicated reference work. I was working at a third-level reference center. One of the member libraries referred this question to us: "An elderly patron wants to know what date (in the early years of this century) a dirigible collided with a skyscraper in Chicago." Some librarians might categorize this as "idle speculation" and perhaps assign it a lower priority, but the referral center treated every question the same.

After some checking, I found the answer. About a month later the referring library forwarded a handwritten thank-you note from the patron. The patron's brother had cancer. As a child he had had radioactive thyroid treatments. His doctor wanted to establish the date, and the patron's sister remembered going downtown with her brother for a treatment on the day the dirigible crash occurred.

The rewards for this involvement in the reference process are tremendous. It is hard for me to imagine another opportunity for satisfaction in our profession equal to the feeling you get when some incredible burst of inspiration sends you straight to the right answer—particularly in a place no one else might have thought to look. This fulfillment and the rapport and feedback that you occasionally get from someone you have helped when you know you have really "made their day" can make up for a lot of stress and drudgery.

Chapter 13

Literary Connections

At least one novel has been published without using the letter *e*. What is the title?

A work published without using a specific letter or letters is called a lipogram, which suggests that the practice is not entirely unknown. The longest English entry in this field, as far as we know, is *Gadsby: A Story of Over 50,000 Words Without Using the Letter E* (Wright, 1939). An Associated Press item in the *Chattanooga Times* (1939) gives some background:

> To write a readable novel containing not a single letter "e," the author should have not only perseverance, but some sort of a bromide preparation handy. . . . Wright worked on the book five and a half months, tieing down the "e" bar of his typewriter. He wrote it to prove that "e," commonly used five times more than any other letter, is not indispensable. . . . The 67-year-old Wright, a Bostonian and a naval musician in the World War, wrote "Gadsby" at the National Military Home in Los Angeles. He died at the home October 7, just as the first review copies came off the presses.

Here is a brief sample from the novel:

> Gadsby was walking back from a visit down in Branton Hill's manufacturing district on a Saturday night. A busy day's traffic had had its noisy run; and with not many folks in sight, His Honor got along without having to stop to grasp a hand, or talk; for a Mayor of City Hall is a shining mark for any politician. And so, coming to Broadway, a booming bass drum and sounds of singing, told of a small Salvation Army unit carrying on amidst Broadway's night shopping crowds. (Wright, 1939)

There is also a French novel written without the letter "e," by Georges Perec (1969), titled *La Disparition*. This book was "so well written that some critics praised it without noticing anything strange" (Gardner, 1977). Several books of the *Odyssey of Tryphiodorus* are lipograms, in which the first book has no "a" and the second no "b," etc. (*Century Dictionary,* 1906).

One of the most interestingly titled books that a patron wanted was *The Schmalhausen Complex; or the Erotic Nature of Odd Shaped Apartments.*

Unfortunately, the Schmalhausen title does not exist apart from a few references in *Is Sex Necessary* (Thurber and White, 1929; Miller, 1982).

In "The Devil and Daniel Webster," by Stephen Vincent Benét, there is a character named the Reverend John Smeet. Was this a real person?

Mrs. Stephen Vincent Benét (1960), in a letter to *The New York Times Book Review,* claimed that the good reverend was entirely imaginary. Mrs. Benét explained that her husband occasionally used to insert imaginary people in his writings. Benét even quoted from a made-up person named John Cleveland Cotton. He went so far as to write an apocryphal biographical note about Cotton that ended up in Marion King's *Books and People* (King, 1954). In this Benét anticipated authors Tom Powers and James Blaylock, who created a poet named William Ashbless (see p. 126).

Why is the Apocrypha omitted from the King James or Authorized Version of the Bible?

There are three reasons why the Apocrypha is usually omitted. The first is theological. Early Reformation Protestants came to believe that the Apocrypha held no divine authority for Christians, although it continued to be translated into English. Parts of the Apocrypha were included in the early English translations of the Bible (Wycliffe, Coverdale, Tyndale) as well as the Authorized Version. The Calvinists on the Continent and England tended to accept the Hebrew canon, which excluded the Apocrypha. By the 1640s, because of their influence, many editions of the Bible were being printed that omitted the Apocrypha.

This practical rejection of them found expression in 1827, in the action of the British and American Bible Societies declining to use any of the funds given them in publishing the Apocrypha. Most printings of the King James Bible during the century that followed omitted them, and now it is difficult to find the Apocrypha in any English Bibles except those designed for pulpit use. (Goodspeed, 1939)

The most common practice is to publish the Apocrypha separately from the canonical books of the Bible. The Roman Catholic Church recognizes the Apocrypha as canonical, and the Rheims, Douai, Jerusalem, and other versions authorized by the Church continue to retain the Apocrypha.

The second reason is more pragmatic. Paper and printing were expensive, and early publishers were able to hold down costs by eliminating the Apocrypha once it was deemed secondary material. Third, the Apocrypha of the Authorized Version is the weakest part of the translation, and newer, more authoritative translations are given precedence by publishers (Taylor, 1989; Greenslade, 1963; Eadie, 1876; Price, 1956).

Where can a copy of "The Declaration of Feminism" be found?
This is something that Pat Robertson supposedly has referred to, and, according to responses to "The Exchange," can be found in a periodical titled *Gold Flower; A Twin Cities Newspaper for Women.* A supposed date of issue is December 1971/January 1972. A book titled *Before It's Too Late* (Jeremiah, 1982) includes some extracts from the alleged document, listing the authors of the "Declaration" as Nancy Lehmann and Helen Sullinger.

What is the title of a novel in which Shakespeare's plays were actually written by a woman who was part of the actor's company at the Globe Theatre?
This is probably *Dark Lady* by Cothburn O'Neal (1954). The plot concerns Rosaline deVere, the illegitimate daughter of the Earl of Oxford, who wrote "Shakespearian" sonnets and plays. To protect her identity, an actor named Shakespeare agreed to issue the works under his name.

What is the title of the short story that deals with an elderly woman, a former concert pianist, who hallucinates that her cat is the incarnation of Franz Liszt?

While not the exact plot, a very similar story by Roald Dahl is titled "Edward the Conqueror." In this story, a woman character (not a former concert pianist but a competent pianist and a genuine music lover) believes a cat that has wandered into her yard is a reincarnation of Franz Liszt. The story appeared in *The New Yorker* and in an anthology, *Kiss, Kiss* (Dahl, 1953, 1960).

How is "black humor" defined?

The concept of black humor is discussed in an article titled "Those Clowns of Conscience" (Friedman, 1965). Other good sources are: *The World of Black Humor* (Davis, 1967); "Laughter in the Dark: The New Voice in American Fiction" (Hassan, 1964); *The Fabulators* (Scholes, 1967); and "American Humor, 1966" (Zinsser, 1966).

What is the title of the novel about a pope who wanted J. S. Bach canonized?

This is a book by Johannes Ruber (1973), published in Germany with the title *Die Heiligsprechung des Johann Sebastian Bach*. There is an English translation by Maurice Michael (Ruber, 1956) and a paperback edition published in 1964. Both editions had the title *Bach and the Heavenly Choir*.

What was the origin of the famous child's book review, which read simply, "This book tells me more about penguins than I wanted to know"?

H. Allen Smith's *Write Me a Poem, Baby* includes this passage:

> One of the most widely quoted bits of preadolescent writing is a letter from a ten-year-old girl to a children's book club. The club had sent a child a volume about penguins, enclosing a card urging her to express her opinion of it. She wrote, "This book gives me more information about penguins than I care to have." The late Hugh Gibson, who served both the government and the book world, described the letter as the finest piece of literary criticism he had ever read. (Smith, 1956)

Who was the author of a children's story about a family named Apple?

Mr. Apple's Family is a story about a family that named its children after varieties of apples (McDevitt, 1950). Two of the children probably would not have been teased (Jonathan and Ann), but what about MacIntosh, Delicious, and Snow?

Since interest in gladiators periodically resurfaces, it is appropriate to include a request for the prose recitation that begins: "You call me chief and you do well to call him chief who for twelve long years fought every sort of man and beast the Empire of Rome could produce."

This is from a long prose piece by E. Kellogg titled "Spartacus to the Gladiators at Capua." The entire text can be found in *A Treasury of the Familiar* (Woods, 1942).

Another oration remembered from parental recitations described someone called Aunt Hettie Tarbox. Who was Hettie?

> Aunt Hettie Tarbox was as cheerful a person as you could find in a Sabbath day's journey. Yet it was only when you put a needle in her hand or a cutting board on her lap that her memory started on its endless journey through the fields of the past.

This oration is from Scene X in *Timothy's Quest* (Wiggin, 1895). It was located through *Granger's Index,* in the 1904 and 1918 editions. This is a good argument for not discarding older editions of sources such as *Granger's.*

There was a story or a ballad with the title "The Prentice Pillar." It has something to do with a church in a Scottish village. What information is available on this pillar?

The pillar is in the chapel of Rosslyn Castle (Mackey, 1946). It is located in Midlothian, Scotland. The Prentice Pillar, one of the internal columns, is carved with rich foliage designs that spiral around the column. The quality and beauty of the pillar's decoration is such that it has developed a tradition all of its own. The legend relates the story of the master mason at Rosslyn, who went to Italy to study the original for the proposed design. While he was absent, his apprentice, having dreamed that he had finished the pillar, carried out the final carving work on a much grander scale than originally envisioned. On his return, the master mason was so enraged with envy that he picked up a hammer and threw it at the apprentice. The apprentice died from the blow.

One troublesome question that frequently reoccurs at reference desks is a request for bibliographic verification of *The Book of Counted Sorrows,* which Dean Koontz sometimes uses as a "source" for introductory quotations in his books.

This question has caused many librarians countless fruitless hours in searches. Finally, Koontz took to sending out postcards explaining that he made up the title and apologizing for leading librarians astray. Koontz did place an advertisement in *Locus* noting that someone had produced a sixty-page book of poetry titled *The Book of Counted Sorrows.* Koontz said he intended at some point to publish his material in a book with that title and considered the prior publication a copyright infringement (Anderson, 1994). Koontz has been getting 3,000 to 4,000 letters a year from fans asking how to get the book and finally produced an e-book, published by Barnes and Noble in 2001 (Koontz, 2001).

Here is one more literary myth. Authors Tim Powers and James Blaylock have, upon occasion, referred to a poet named William Ashbless in their books. Librarians searching for biographical information about Ashbless will embark on a fruitless search.

Like *The Book of Counted Sorrows,* William Ashbless never existed. When Powers and Blaylock were in college, they collaborated on deliberately bad poetry and were able to publish it in the college paper under the name William Ashbless. When they became professional writers, they quoted him in their books independently, which led to some problems with chronology (Helgesen, 1991).

Who was Zoe Cass?

At the time this question was asked, the only information available suggested that Cass was the pseudonym of "a well-known author." Now, when one does a Web search on this name, the *Romantic Times* site suggests that it may be a real name with several pseudonyms attached (Dorothy Mackie Low and Lois Paxton).

Neither the Library of Congress nor Dr. Seuss himself could provide a copy of "Ode to a Zode," and "The Exchange" was asked to help.

An "Exchange" reader scanned the word "zode" on OCLC and found an analytic entry under "The Zode" by Dr. Seuss. This led to a location in a book titled *Developing Student Leaders* (Johnston, 1992).

Who wrote and drew the comic book series "Little Boy Blue"?

Little Boy Blue and the Blue Boys first appeared in National Periodical Publications' (today's Comics, Inc.) *Sensation Comics*, no. 1, January 1942. The comic strip continued publication through no. 83, November 1948. The characters also appeared in *The Big All-American Comic Book* in 1944 and *Flash Comics* in March 1947. Little Boy Blue was Tommy Rogers, son of Big City District Attorney Dan Rogers, and the Blue Boys were two of his friends, Tubby and Toughy. As costumed crimefighters, inspired by the proliferation of "mystery men" of the day, the trio had no super powers but triumphed over their foes through cleverness and athletic skill (Wein, 1986; Bails, 1969). No specific artist was identified by readers.

There is a novel with a character named Risper. What is the title and who is the author of this book?

Although the novel was never identified, the name Risper probably came either from Tennyson's poem "Rispah" (Walsh, 1914) or from a biblical reference: "and Saul had a concubine whose name was Rispah, the daughter of Ajah" (Gormley, 1987).

What is the source of the title of Peter Matthiessen's *At Play in the Fields of the Lord?*

This appears to be a play on an old missionary phrase—"At work in the fields of the Lord" (Morse, 1965).

What novel includes people called we-ans?

This is from a book by Robert Nathan, titled *The Weans*. It is an archaeological parody concerning the interpretation of American civilization 5,000 years in the future. The term "weans" refers to the discovery by future archaeologists of references to a land called US (Nathan, 1960).

A Celtic studies group was trying to trace research compiled by Russian and Eastern European folklorists, anthropologists, and

musicologists on pre-Christian religions that still existed as late as World War I in areas of Latvia, Lithuania, and Estonia.

In addition to material in specialized encyclopedias (Hastings, 1951; Eliade, 1987), a book on Latvian folk songs was suggested as a source (Vikis-Freibergs, 1989).

What is the title of a story about friendship in which one of two friends is sentenced to be executed? His last wish is a visit home. His friend takes his place in prison with the proviso that if the prisoner does not return in the allotted time, his friend will have to be executed.

The story of Damon and Pythias is the source of this supreme example of friendship (Benét, 1987). Besides the Greek legend, this theme appears in other literature. One example is an Edward Arnold translation of an Arabian legend, "Al-Maumin." In this story, a sheik is captured and sentenced to death. The sheik asks to be allowed to return home to see his newborn son before the sentence is carried out. A nephew offers himself as a hostage. When the sheik is late returning, the nephew is almost executed in his place. However, like Pythias, the sheik returns in time and both parties are freed.

What is a carker? It is something that comes into a short story set in the southwestern United States in an abandoned house.

Carkers are small creatures who eat people in a story by Anthony Boucher titled "They Bite." Boucher was the pseudonym of William Anthony Parker White (1911-1968), who was a reviewer of detective novels and a founding father of *The Magazine of Fantasy and Science Fiction*. The story first appeared in 1943, but it can be found in several anthologies: *A Treasury of Modern Fantasy; Dying of Fright; Great Black Magic Stories;* and *Alfred Hitchcock Presents My Favorites in Suspense.*

Who is the children's illustrator who drew Mr. and Mrs. Limpid?

This is from a Tomi Ungerer book titled, *I Am Papa Snap and These Are My Favorite No Such Stories* (Ungerer, 1971).

The opening sentence in a standard textbook on rural sociology, probably published in the 1930s or 1940s, reads "An educated civi-

lization, not an ignorant population, should be built upon the fertile soil of America." What was the title and who wrote this book?

"A rural civilization, not a peasant population, should be built upon the fertile soil of America" is the opening sentence of *The Sociology of Rural Life* by Horace Hawthorn (1926). This question took over six years to answer, a tribute to some reference librarian's dogged persistence!

There is a fairy tale/folktale/children's story concerning a girl who is unhappy with her legs. She goes to a room where all shapes and sizes of legs can be found. After much searching, she chooses her own. What is this story?

The title of this story is "Once Upon a Time" and it can be found in *Fairy Tales and Other Stories* (1929).

Once upon a time there was a card game called Authors. Are copies still available?

This game is still available from U.S. Games Systems Inc. The company has a Web site at <http://www.usgamesinc.com>. The mailing address is 179 Ludlow Street, Stamford, CT 06902. The game was invented in the 1860s by August A. Smith.

James Thurber, E. B. White, or possibly Robert Benchley wrote a humorous essay in which the narrator is befuddled by the dialect of a hired man. The piece may be called "The Hired Hand."

This may be James Thurber's "The Black Magic of Barney Haller" (Thurber, 1957).

There was a book or article titled *Diary of an Unknown Aviator.* Where can a copy be found?

This is the subtitle of *War Birds,* a book by John McGavock Grider (1926). The Library of Congress subject heading is "European War, 1914-1918—Personal narratives, American."

A short story describes the visit to the Tomb of the Unknown Soldier by parents who lost a son in World War I. They laid a wreath at the tomb and suddenly yellow butterflies flew away from the grave. **They felt this was a sign their son was buried there. What is the title of this story and who wrote it?**

The title is *Yellow Butterflies,* and it was written by Mary Raymond (Shipman) Andrews. It was published by Scribner's in 1922 in a small book format of seventy-three pages.

Chapter 14

Reference Anxiety

Does any of the following describe your feelings lately? If so, you maybe suffering symptoms of a modern, but previously uncataloged, syndrome called Reference Anxiety. I've made a close study of this condition and have come to the following conclusions (in the format of the *Merck Manual of Diagnosis and Therapy*).

Classification and Etiology

Further research is needed to develop staging categories for this condition, although the degree of severity seems to be related to the length of time since receiving an MLS degree. The condition itself tends to be directly correlated with the duration of exposure to the causative agent, i.e., service at a busy public reference desk. After constant answering of reference questions for a period exceeding two hours, the syndrome manifests itself to some degree in all but the most phlegmatic of individuals. It is probably caused by excessive channeling of information between printed or electronic formats and library users. Reference Anxiety is exacerbated by repetitive requests, irritable users, telephones, malfunctioning computers, and lagging network response times.

Symptoms and Signs

Tendency to make flat statements such as the following: "If one more person asks me why we don't have out-of-state telephone books, I'll scream!" "Is the telephone *ever* going to stop ringing?" "Why can't a teacher ever warn us about an assignment?" "Oh, no, not her [him] again!" A definite harried look may appear on the face. Telephones may be hung up with more violence than usual.

Treatment

The therapy of choice is to remove the individual from the reference desk for at least one hour for every two hours on duty. The maximum safe level of exposure to fast-paced public reference service should be 50 percent of the working day. Emergency relief may be obtained by a simple technique (however, the following method, if overused, tends to lose its effectiveness). When the patient feels an attack of Reference Anxiety coming on, he or she should immediately begin writing obscene words upon the roof of the mouth with the tongue. Although only palliative, this treatment is simple, easily learned, and, with the proper practice, completely unnoticeable to the public. The technique was highly recommended by Peter DeVries in a book in which a pastor was the protagonist and used the technique to maintain sanity when braced by difficult parishioners.

Prognosis

After three hours without relief, the condition tends to worsen. Prolonged exposure without a break from the reference desk may lead to frayed tempers, ulcers (mental if not physical), and errors in the provision of information. Complete recovery is likely; however, there have been cases that proceeded to the dread and sometimes incurable *burnout*.

Chapter 15

Miscellany

How did lullabies begin?

Most lullabies probably originated among the peasantry and working classes, since aristocratic mothers seldom spent much time with their babies. Only the sound and rhythms were important to the babies, because many of the words were incomprehensible. This was for the best, as the images would frighten a child who understood them. The thought of a cradle rocking in a tree would scare any infant (Commins, 1967).

Why is a yawn contagious when sneezing or coughing (unless you catch the other person's cold) is not?

This question was part of a larger study on the ethological basis of yawning by a University of Maryland psychologist, Robert Provine (Provine, 1996). Provine has published extensively on subjects such as yawning and laughing (Provine, n.d.). Actually, as one reader of "The Exchange," pointed out, anyone who has been in a quiet theater and heard the first cough would say that coughing is just as contagious as yawning. For additional information, see Provine's Web site at <http://www.umbc.edu/psyc/faculty/provine/>.

Around the end of the 1800s, some churches operated trains called church trains or chapel cars. Where can I find more information about these?

The service was sponsored by the American Baptist Assembly and operated from 1891 to 1946. The terms used to refer to these church trains are "church-on-rails" or "chapel cars." There were seven cars that ran on the Northern Pacific Railroad. Only two of the seven, *Grace* and *Emmanuel,* are still in existence today. One is on display at the Greenlake Conference Center, Green Lake, Wisconsin (McKeon,

1975; for additional information, see Jennings, 1991; Jones, 1991; Smith, 1991; Willard, 1991).

What is the Eleventh Commandment?

Possibly I John 2:8-9, which reads, "Again, a new commandment I write unto you, which thing is true in him and in you, because the darkness is past, and the true light now shineth. He that saith he is in the light, and hateth his brother, is in darkness even until now" (KJV). Another possibility is Deuteronomy 19:14, "Thou shalt not remove thy neighbour's landmark" (KJV) (Neilson, 1933).

What is the date of the Immaculate Conception?

The following entry from *The Catholic Fact Book* (Deedy, n.d.) may shed some light on this:

> The Vatican lately placed in circulation a new 500-lire silver coin commemorating the 2000th anniversary of the birth of the Blessed Virgin. Issued in 1985, the coin was dated 1984, and led to speculation among some that the Vatican was dating Mary's year of birth as 16 B.C.—a year arrived at by mathematical deduction based on the then-custom of Jewish maidens being pledged in marriage about age 14, with marriage and a shared life following a year or so later.

Extrapolating forward, then, would give an approximate date of around 1 B.C. for the Immaculate Conception. Pope Pius IX defined the dogma of the Immaculate Conception on December 8, 1854, although the feast was observed as early as the eighth century *(Catholic Almanac)*.

Where can I find a copy of an inspirational piece titled "Footprints"?

This was found on a greeting card with no further attribution (Peterson, 1990) and reads:

> One night I dreamed I was walking along the beach with the Lord. I turned and looked back and saw all the footsteps I had taken in my life. Most of the time there were two sets of footprints in the sand—mine and the Lord's. But I noted that sometimes there was only one set of footprints, and these were the

times when the path was steep and rough. So I asked Him, "I thought you would always be with me, Lord. But at the most difficult times in my life, I see only one set of footprints. Why did you leave me when I needed you most?" The Lord answered gently, "I was always with you, my child. Where you see just one set of footprints, I was carrying you."

What was the curse of the monks of Lacroma?

Lacroma is an island near Dubrovnik in Yugoslavia. There was a Benedictine monastery on the island in the twelfth century. When "General Marmont took over the government of Ragusa for Napoleon, he wanted the island for the erection of a fortress, and he turned out the Benedictines. Before they left, they encircled the island and, with bell, book and candle, they put a solemn curse upon it and upon those who should hold it after them" (Ball, 1932). Those who followed turned out be some unhappy Habsburgs, including the Archduke Maximilian and Franz Ferdinand, both of whom met violent deaths. Further verification may be found in a book referenced in an *Encyclopedia Britannica* (1910) article; however, the book appears to be quite rare (Stephanie, 1892).

What and where is the Black Madonna?

A Black Madonna or Black Virgin is "a statue (less often a picture) of Our Lady which is black in color, either because of the material of which it is made, or the way in which it is painted, or on account of age" (Attwater, 1956). The blackness may be caused by smoke from candles offered by countless pilgrims over the ages (Raybould, n.d.). The Black Madonna of Dzestochowa was recovered by monks in the fifteenth century from Hussite raiders who had buried it in earth and blood (Aradi, 1954).

What was the movie *The Texas Chain Saw Massacre* based upon?

The movie was partially based on a 1957 murder case involving a Wisconsin farmer named Edward Gein (Phelps, 1976). A book on Gein was authored by Robert Gollmar (1981).

What were the names of the monkeys in *The Wizard of Oz*?

In the original edition of the work by Frank Baum, the winged monkeys did not have specific names. In *The Magic of Oz,* three nonwinged monkeys are called Ebu, Peeker, and Rango (the "Chief"). In *The Tin*

Woodman of Oz there is a boy named Woot who is temporarily turned into a nonwinged green monkey (Englund, 1984).

Why do pigeons bob their heads when they walk?

Pigeons cannot adjust their focus when moving. Consequently, they stop moving their heads between steps, much like a camera taking a series of snapshots (*TV Guide,* 1983).

How did the game of tiddlywinks get started?

The game was invented by Joseph Assheton Fincher in 1888. Presumably he took the name from a kind of pub called a "kiddleywink," which had become a place of idleness. The game became a worldwide fad in the 1890s. Cambridge University students in 1954 developed tournament tiddlywinks. The tournament game spread to other colleges and was introduced to the United States in 1962. The Massachusetts Institute of Technology won the first world team championship in 1972. Tournament tiddlywinks is now governed by the English Tiddlywinks Association (ETwA) and the North American Tiddlywinks Association (NATwA) (Shapiro, 1986).

What are the rules for military whist?

Military whist is a variation of military euchre, so named because a small flag is transferred from table to table along with the winning side. The Hebron Community Church in Hebron, Maine, for many years sponsored a military whist game at least once a year. Each table has four players—two of whom are partners for scoring purposes—but they may be assigned entirely different tables at each hand, sometimes returning to their original seats for the last hand. The trump is called arbitrarily by the leader. Sometimes losers take the flags; sometimes the command is "play to lose." Unlike bridge, there is no dummy, but the hands are played as at bridge (Fitzpatrick, 1975).

"Y Day" was the name given to the German invasion of Poland on September 1, 1939. The code to attack was given as "Y = 1.9.0445," that is, 4:45 a.m., September 1, 1939. Did "Y" represent a word?

The *Marshall Cavendish Illustrated Encyclopedia of World War II* (1985) confirms this abbreviation does refer to the German invasion of Poland. However, the *Simon and Schuster Encyclopedia of World War II* (1978) and *World War II Super Facts* (McCombs and Worth, 1983) state that Y Day referred to the target date of June 1, 1944, by which time Eisenhower had ordered preparations for the Normandy invasion completed. As a sideline, "Y Service" was the British code name for the interception of enemy radio and telephone traffic.

Are there any published rules for bumper pool?

The rules can be found in *Official Rules and Record Book* (1980) by the Billiards Congress of America and *Popular Mechanics* (1970). One source is the Valley Company, a manufacturer of bumper pool tables, whose address is P.O. Box 656, 333 Morton St., Bay City, MI 48707. The rules are now available on the Web.

When was the "year without a summer"?

If you want to get an understanding of what nuclear winter might be like, you could read a book about the year without a summer. This is described in a book titled *Volcano Weather: The Story of 1816, the Year Without a Summer* (Stommel and Stommel, 1983). On April 5, 1815, Mount Tambora, on the island of Sumbawa in Indonesia, began erupting. It was the most explosive eruption of a volcano in 10,000 years. For comparison, Mount St. Helens and Vesuvius ejected one cubic kilometer of material, Krakatoa ejected ten cubic kilomters, and Mount Tambora 100 cubic kilometers. Ashes were carried as far as 300 miles away, and floating cinders on the ocean west of Sumatra formed a mass two feet thick and several miles in diameter.

The clouds from the eruption of Mount Tambora dispersed around the world. This caused such severe weather that in 1816, when the clouds reached the East Coast of the United States, it caused the year without a summer. During the period of May through September, 1816, arctic blasts devastated much of the northeastern United States. In Williamstown, Massachusetts, it was 30.5 degrees on June 11. In June, snow fell as far south as western Massachusetts. On August 20 temperatures in New Hampshire dropped 30 degrees. Almost all the corn and other staple crops died. Famine in the United States and Western Europe was severe.

Is there a scientific term for sunrise?

The scientific definition for sunrise:

> The times at which the apparent upper limb of the sun is on the astronomical horizon, i.e., when the true zenith distance, referred to the center of the earth, of the central point of the disk is

90 degrees 50 minutes, based on adopted values of 34 minutes for horizontal refraction and 16 minutes for the Sun's semi diameter. (*Astronomical Almanac,* 1982)

What is the circumference of the earth at 45 degrees latitude?

Simple geometry produces an answer of 28,337 kilometers, but it took an "Exchange" reader to work out the method (Tyckoson, 1980).

What flowers are used to create "flower clocks," U-shaped gardens popular in the 1800s?

These gardens were planted with specific flowers so that when one type opened, the one behind it closed—all of this taking place on an hourly basis. Lesley Gordon (1977) wrote a book titled *Green Magic: Flowers, Plants, and Herbs in Lore and Legend* that lists flowers to use in a clock garden.

What is known about the origins of the peace symbol?

The generally accepted origin is the Aldermaston Easter Peace Walk in 1958. Gerald Holton, who created the sign, states that it was designed on February 21, 1958, and immediately adopted by Hugh Brock and Pat Arrowsmith on behalf of the Direct Action Committee Against Nuclear War (Holton, 1971). This was the group that initiated and organized the first Aldermaston march.

Since the words "Unilateral Nuclear Disarmament" took up so much space on a banner, Holton created a symbol based on a combination of the semaphore signs for N and D (nuclear disarmament). There may well be deeper motifs. For example, some have seen the center as an ancient symbol for man dying and the circle representing eternity or the unborn child (Greer, 1962).

An apocryphal version sees a connection to evil—a sign of the Christian cross with the crossbars broken down to symbolize Satan's contempt for Christian purposes (*Evening Observer,* 1970). However, the source for this, supposedly *The New Yorker,* turned out to be false. The actual article quoted in this newspaper report appears to have come from something called the *Western Police News* (1971). *The New Yorker* denied ever printing an article on the peace symbol (Schweik, 1970).

Years ago, when the Skylab satellite fell, people watched the summer skies with increased interest and not a little concern. It

brought to mind in at least one reader a story about a Nicaraguan general named Pablo Castilliano who, while sitting in his tent after a victorious battle, was killed by a meteor. Did this really happen?

Although it was never confirmed, a reader supplied some calculations of the likelihood of such an event, which might be worth keeping in mind:

> The earth gains about 400×10^6 grams (about 400 tons) of mass each day in meteorite material, but nearly all of it is in the form of dust-size particles which do no harm. It is estimated that only two meteors per day are big enough to impact and potentially damage something. Suppose the size of each is 10 cm. Since the area of the earth is 5×10^{18} cm² the probability that any square centimeter of the earth's surface will suffer meteor impact is about 2×10^{-17} for any given day. Assuming that a person may have a cross-sectional area of about 1,000 cm², if a person could be anywhere on the earth's surface (including anywhere at sea), the probability that he/she would be hit by a meteor is about 2×10^{-14} per day. In plainer terms, if you were waiting for a meteor to hit you, you should be prepared to wait at least 10 billion years. (Bopp, 1979)

Continuing with the possible disaster motif, one reader wondered why tornadoes appear to seek out trailer parks.

Completely unsubstantiated answers included the following, proving that even reference librarians have a sense of humor:

- Trailers, sitting on concrete blocks, are more easily tossed about than houses anchored to foundations.
- If trailers didn't exist, would tornadoes exist?
- Tornadoes need to eat aluminum trailers as a good source of energy and vitamins.

What is the origin of the tea bag?

Although *The Book of Firsts* (Robertson, 1974) gives credit to Joseph Krieger of San Francisco, several other sources say that Thomas Sullivan, a stingy merchant of New York, invented them (Kaufman, 1966; Shalleck, 1972; Trager, 1970). Varying dates for the first use are given—1904 and 1908. Sullivan's motive appears to have been entirely commercial. He sent out tea samples in little silk bags instead of larger tins. Then he started getting orders for the silk bags, not for the tea they contained.

What is the origin of the Chinese water torture?

This practice started in the Middle Ages and not necessarily in China according to some encyclopedia entries.

What is the word for the science of beer brewing?

"Fermentology" would cover this, although it is broader in the sense of dealing with fermentation in the context of alcoholic beverages. There is also "zymurgy" (Helgesen, 1991; Urdang, 1986).

What are the vital statistics of the Venus de Milo?

Different sources give slightly different measurements. For example, an article in *Horizon* (Rudolfsky, 1971) endowed the Venus with a 37-26-38 figure. An authoritative list in meters came directly from the Louvre: Height, 2.02; bust, with right arm, 1.33; upper right arm, 0.41; waist, 0.985; hips, 1.21; circumference of head at forehead, 0.653; neck, 0.48; length of face, 0.198; width of shoulders, across back, 0.55; width of back at armpits, 0.52; length of foot, 0.31 (Pasquier, 1975).

What is the name and the history of the medal featured in the movie *The Blue Max*?

The medal is called Pour le Mérite and is roughly equivalent to our Congressional Medal of Honor or the British Victoria Cross. It was established by Frederick the Great. German air aces were unhappy that a German decoration was known by a French name. They nicknamed Prince Frederick "Max," a derogatory nickname, for giving it the name Pour le Mérite (Hunter, 1983).

What is the current composition of a penny, and when did this change?

In fiscal year 1982 the copper-plated zinc cent was phased in, and the composition changed from 95 percent copper, 5 percent zinc to 97.5 percent copper, 2.5 percent zinc (*Annual Report*, 1982).

What was the name of the piece used as a signature theme by the BBC's *Masterpiece Theatre*?

The music is "Rondeau" from Joseph Mouret's *Suite de symphonie, no. 1* (Mouret, n.d.).

There is a management training exercise called the Ugli Orange Case. Where can some information on this case be found?

A description of this exercise appears in *Group and Organization Management* (Butler, 1995). Full information on the case can be found in *Experiences in Management and Organizational Behavior* (Lewicki et al., 1988).

What is the significance of "a quarter of three"? Is there any connection to the common belief that a group of people automatically fall silent at twenty minutes past (or before) each hour?

Friedrich Engels (1883) gave a speech at the graveside of Karl Marx in which he said, "On the fourteenth of March, at a quarter to three in the afternoon, the greatest living thinker ceased to think." Another theory holds that 2:45 is significant mainly because at that time the hands of an analog clock are very nearly horizontal. *More of the Straight Dope* (Adams, 1988) discusses the aesthetic value of the 8:20 and 10:10 settings frequently seen on clocks in catalogs. Finally, "The Last Prophet" by Mildred Clingerman (Boucher, n.d.), turns on the idea that twenty minutes past the hour is hardwired into the human mind as a quiet time to listen for God's return.

What libraries serve as last resting places for individuals?

Langston Hughes' remains are interred beneath the floor of the Schomburg Library in Harlem (Scilken, 1995). The ashes of Nicola Sacco and Bartolomeo Vanzetti, executed in 1927 for the robbery of a Massachusetts shoe company in which two people were killed, were donated to the Boston Public library after Governor Michael Dukakis signed a proclamation in 1977 clearing their names (Bender and Zepp, 1995).

The Coconut Grove Branch Library (Miami-Dade Library System) has "the loneliest grave in Dade County." There is an isolated grave right at the entrance to the library. Eva Amelia Munroe (1856-1882) has been resting there since 1896, when she was moved from another site that had a church and a planned cemetery. When the Coconut Grove branch was built, it turned out that the boundary line between the site of the old cemetery (later an American Legion Hall) and the library passed right through the grave site. So the city acquired an additional five feet of property and preserved the grave (Boldrick, 1995).

Dr. James Rion McKissick (1884-1944), president of the University of South Carolina at Columbia from 1936 to his death, is buried just a few feet from the main entrance to the Caroliniana Library (Evatt, 1995). Robert Bloch (author of *Psycho* and many other books), who died in 1994, requested that he be cremated and his ashes kept in a book-shaped urn at the University of Wyoming (Folkhart, 1994).

One patron tried the local library to find information about a ring. The ring belonged to a man in his eighties and had the initials FLT in white, blue, and red interlocking circles. The circles had notches on each side. When the library exhausted its own resources they turned to "The Exchange."

The 1897 Sears, Roebuck catalog answered this question. The ring was from the Odd Fellows organization. The letters stood for Friendship, Love, and Truth (Israel, 1968).

Who were the Gleaners?

The Gleaners was an organization for young ladies in the Church of Jesus Christ of Latter-Day Saints. Similarly named groups of young ladies were part of other church groups (Strain, 1977).

What kind of musical instrument is a *krotar*?

This is probably a misspelling for crotala, a sort of castanet (Sadie, 1984).

What is the initial velocity of a golf ball?

The launch velocity of a golf ball is between 215 and 240 feet per second (146 to 164 miles per hour) (Evans, 1974). The U.S. Golf Association says "the maximum speed of the ball shall not be greater than 250 feet per second" (Scharff, 1973).

At what rate are different languages spoken?

Some averages given in *The Story of Language* (Pei, 1965) are: French, 350 syllables per minute; English, 220 syllables per minute; and South Sea languages, 50 syllables per minute. Pei goes on to say that American men speak at 150 words per minute and American women at 175 words per minute.

What is the significance of the *matrimony vine*?

"The Exchange" did not receive any authoritative answers to this, although one writer opined that it might be because the plant is so thorny! The plant is a toxin belonging to the nightshade family.

What is the probability of finding a double-yoked egg?

Extensive research, including consultations with the American Egg Board and the National Dairy Council, resulted in several answers. This is a more complex question than it seems. Depending on variables such as age, weight, when laying begins, and genetic selection, there may be a frequency ranging from two to twenty-nine double-yoked eggs during a forty-week laying period. If you are only talking about one chicken, given the average number of eggs laid by a hen in fifty-two weeks (238.7), assuming that a minimum of two of these were double-yoked, then the odds would be 100 to 1 (Anderson, 1983).

Why does a seagull have a red spot on its beak?

This functions as a "releaser" at the first chick feeding. It stimulates the hungry chicks to pick at the parental bill (*Grzimek's,* 1972).

Do hummingbirds hitchhike?

These birds are not hitchhiking; rather, they are resting on the back of another bird before resuming a vigorous attack on that bird (*The Washington Star,* 1958, 1959). The scientific name for nonparasitic relationships in which one species is carried about by another is "phoresy", but this description would not fit that term.

How did someone come up with the "Rule of 72" for interest accumulation?

It is called the Rule of 72 because at 1 percent interest it would take seventy-two years for one dollar to grow to two dollars (*Think of Your Future,* 1986).

What major league baseball pitcher won and lost the same game?

There never was a perfect answer to this question. Warren Spahn, a rookie pitcher for the Boston Braves in 1942, was credited with one complete game that season, but he had a 0-0 record in four appearances. In a September 26 doubleheader, Spahn was pitching and was trailing 5-2 in the bottom of the eighth inning, when hundreds of youngsters ran onto the field. They refused to leave, so the umpire, Ziggy Sears, forfeited the game to the Braves 9-0. This resulted in Spahn not being credited with a win, but not a loss either, even if he did get credit for a complete game (Hoppel, 1983).

What was the source of the music played during President Clinton's inauguration?

Marvin Curtis, an associate professor of music and the men's choral director at California State–Stanislaus from 1988 to 1991, was commissioned to write some music for the inauguration. The concept for the music came from the theme "The City on the Hill," the idea of which came from Massachusetts Bay Colony governor John Winthrop in the 1620s (Santos, 1993).

Although the following was not a question received by "The Exchange," it falls into the category of puzzles that were occasionally added to the column for librarians to add to their "hard-to-find" file. Speakers in the information industry or reporters in the popular press at times refer to the doubling of information every *x* number of years. The exact basis of this kind of statement is difficult to establish.

Stumpers-L (a listserv moderated by GSLIS students at Dominican University, Chicago, Illinois) has several items in its archives on this subject. Dennis Lien (University of Minnesota Libraries) posted a reference that may shed more light on this idea. Robert Anton Wilson, in *Cosmic Trigger Vol. II: Down to Earth* writes, "If you use a computer and know the correct algorithms, you can convert anything into binary notation. You can then estimate the information in a mathematical theorem, a painting, a book, or any human product" (Wilson, 1991). In this way, in 1974, according to Wilson, statistician Georges Anderla estimated how much information humanity had accumulated between a prehistoric African stone axe and the beginning of the Christian calendar in 1 A.D. According to Wilson, Anderla calculated that the amount of information up to 1 A.D. had doubled by 1500. Although Wilson did not provide a footnote, Lien suggests a likely source is Georges Anderla, *The Growth of Scientific and Technical Information, a Challenge: Lecture and Seminar Proceedings* (Anderla, 1974). Lien goes on to note that, according to Wilson/

Anderla, the next doubling took 250 years (to 1750), then 150 (to 1900), then fifty (to 1950), then ten (to 1960), then seven (to 1967), then six (to 1973), which is presumably as far as Anderla got. This rate, if extended, means that since I started writing these paragraphs, information probably doubled several times, leaving me to wonder what I missed while composing!

Actually, as others have noted, this whole argument results from confusion between data, information, and knowledge. If one thinks of *data* as meaningless strings of alphanumeric characters bounded by spaces (or pixels, or whatever other medium is in question), *information* is what *data* becomes when it is transferred somehow to a human being who can use it, and *knowledge* is *information* that becomes a part of our culture and corpus of thought, then the doubling of information is not as significant as ways to increase our ability to sort, evaluate, and absorb knowledge.

Chapter 16

Technological Change and Libraries

In the thirty-five years that "The Exchange" tried to find answers to puzzling questions, enormous changes took place in the way that reference services are delivered. On the other hand, as Alphonse Karr, 1808-1890, noted in *Les Guêpes, "Plus ça change, plus c'est la même chose,"* or, colloquially, "been there, done that." One of the questions partially answered in a Winter 1984 column was for the source of the saying about "the whole nine yards." No doubt a source for this quotation is still being requested at some reference desk even as I write—and someone may be searching a Web database for this phrase at this very moment.

In that Winter 1984 issue of *RQ*, the "Databases Reviewed" column covered four databases. In the Summer 1998 issue of *RUSQ*, the same column reviewed five databases—not that big a change. However, in 1984 the databases required mediated searching by a librarian or other trained searcher and had connect hour and per citation charges. For example, Trademarkscan cost $85 per connect hour, plus $.25 per full offline citation or $.15 per online citation. Abstrax cost $80 per connect hour plus $.04 per online citation, or $.25 per offline citation. By 1999, many public library patrons could access and search, at no cost to them, on their own, from home, business, or in the smallest library in the system, a wealth of electronic information.

These are just a few of the changes in the way reference service is provided, and I will not bore the reader with reciting more of the obvious. If these changes had taken place in an orderly, year-by-year fashion, library staff might be a bit more comfortable. We might not hear requests such as, "Couldn't we put a moratorium on change for six months to get used to what we have?" This is not an unusual request, nor does it necessarily indicate isolated instances of Luddism. Reference librarians are, after all, human beings. It is only natural that the stress of ever-increasing change should cause major staff concern. Putting a moratorium on change is like saying, "Can we get off this train and get on the next one?" If you do that, you will never catch up.

Change now is occurring not as it used to, with decade-long spans between the invention of new technology, the gradual development of it, and its final acceptance as commonplace in society. For just one example of this long process, think of commercial aviation in the 1930s and how commonplace travel by air had become by the 1960s. Now think about what we had available for reference services at the start of the 1990s and what we have today. Moreover, these changes were not divided evenly over the past ten years.

Rather, two- to three-year revolutions occurred. Even library systems noted for being on the fast track for technology did not have any Internet links for the public in 1994. In 1995 gateway systems including many links to gophers became more common. Three years later, it is not easy to find a gopher site, and libraries running gateway menus probably have seen these shrink to half-a-dozen or so offerings. Web links, on the other hand, fill up page after page on the public access screens. With the current rate of change more like a logarithmic curve than a straight line, can anyone who thinks seriously about this doubt that in the coming years, our reference world may well be dramatically different than it is today?

Here is one final, albeit lengthy, question that awaits an answer: What are you doing in your library to prepare the staff and the public to adapt to whatever reference services will be like in the new millennium? Have you assumed that from now on, change will continue to be incremental, and you will only need to tweak current services slightly to keep up, i.e., are you taking the path of least resistance? Alternatively, are you forming staff/administrative task forces to take the way of greatest advantage, that is, doing some serious thinking, visioning, and planning? Are public libraries trying to apply some of the research being done in academic libraries such as that described in an article by Rose, Stoklosa, and Gray (1998)? Are you looking at new and proactive ways of reaching people who never physically visit the library but are becoming heavy remote users? For example, how do we provide reference help for someone who tries to find information on a commercial database through the library's Web site (in-house or remotely) but because of a lack of understanding of search strategy, finds less than adequate information? What about users who go directly to a Web search engine, enter a term, get 45,000 hits, and scan the first ten—perhaps finding something useful—but do not realize that some simple qualifiers might retrieve ten times that much useful information? How can we help them?

Chapter 17

Unanswered Questions

Although every reference librarian would certainly like to answer every question that comes their way, we all know this is simply not possible. This is not to say that the popular "50 percent" rule is in operation with every question that comes across the reference desk.

However, no matter how hard we may try, inevitably there are going to be questions that simply cannot be answered in the local library. Various options may exist depending upon the sophistication and resources of the particular library. A multitiered reference support service may be in place within the local area or even within the state. If this type of resource is not available, depending upon the patron's desire to know and the librarian's desire (which includes extrinsic factors such as library policy) to answer the question, various external sources may be tried (I am assuming that the Web has already been tried without success).

One resource of last resort that existed for many years was the various serial publications dealing with odd, unusual questions. A well-known one is the English *Notes and Queries* and its American counterpart, *American Notes and Queries.* Another was a column written especially for reference librarians in *RQ* (later retitled *Reference and User Services Quarterly*) upon which this entire book is based. In later years we had the famous Stumpers electronic mail list as well as search engines for the Web.

The column in *RQ/RUSQ,* titled simply "The Exchange," was read not only in United States but also by librarians in a number of other countries including Japan, India, Australia, New Zealand, and Great Britain. For this reason, when questions that appeared in "The Exchange" were never answered even years and decades later (because some diligent reference librarians continued to pursue questions even after retirement from a library job), one might conclude that they simply do not have an answer.

However, this would be a dangerous assumption. The reason that questions with no answer appear in this final chapter with the heading "Unanswered Questions" is simply to provide a clue to both the reference librarian and the patron that the answer to a particular question may not be available. As every good reference librarian knows, proving a negative is extremely difficult. How many times in the past have you been asked, "Is so-and-so still alive?" If you do not find the person's obituary, can you conclude that the person is still living? Not really—you can only hedge your answer.

With the kinds of questions that fell into the unanswered category in "The Exchange," it would be very difficult to conclude absolutely that no possible answer exists. Indeed, one of the hopes of presenting these unanswered questions in this book is that some reader, somewhere, sometime, may actually have an answer. If so, a revised edition of this book could include these answers. I do believe that having these questions available may at least save some harried reference librarian some time at some point in the future. It seems valid to apply something that Tony Shipps said in *The Quote Sleuth: A Manual for the Tracer of Lost Quotations* to all the questions that appeared in "The Exchange," whether answered or not: "If, as sometimes happens, a query is never answered, it still stands for all time as evidence that someone in need of the source of a quotation did all that was possible to find it" (Shipps, 1990).

With that said, here are the questions that stumped reference librarians on four continents.

Strange and Common Customs

How did the wording on diplomas originate?

What was the origin of high school and college yearbooks, and how did the tradition of signing them begin?

What is the origin of the common gesture—the "shame on you" sign—made by stroking the index finger of one hand with the index finger of the other hand?

Popular Sayings

Here is a list of popular sayings that probably are familiar to many readers. However, during the many years of coverage in "The Exchange" their origins were never uncovered. Perhaps a reader now can shed some light on these adages.

Something old, something new, something borrowed, something blue

Motherhood and apple pie

The luck of the Irish

What goes around, comes around.

That's the way we've always done it.

A man ten feet tall

The Moody's Goose that Tennessee Ernie Ford used to refer to on his TV show

When a woman is alone there are four things she must do: dress like a girl, act like a lady, think like a man, and work like a horse.

Patch hell a mile.

Curiosity killed the cat: Satisfaction brought it back!

Things may come to those who wait, but only the things left by those who hustle.

Chinese auction

God willing and the creek don't rise.

Quotations

The first thing to keep in mind with quotation hunts is some advice offered in *The Quote Sleuth: A Manual for the Tracer of Lost Quotations* (Shipps, 1990):

Time spent looking for quotations is never wasted.

A one-line quotation may be the first line of a poem.

A one-line quotation may be the last line of a poem.

The *Oxford English Dictionary* is a book of quotations.

With those helpful aphorisms in mind, here are some quotations still open for solutions:

I'd rather get to hell late than to Chicago on time.

Never trust a man with two first names.

Never trust a man who parts his hair down the middle.

Another life perhaps. The power that brought us here would lead us there.

When love and skill work together, expect a masterpiece.

George Bernard Shaw is credited with saying, "Youth is a wonderful thing. What a crime it is to waste it on children." Where exactly in Shaw's works can this be found?

Knowledge maketh a bloody entrance.

The hub is the part of the wheel that moves the slowest.

Mark Twain supposedly said, "The man who does not read good books has no advantage over the man who can't read them." What is the exact source of this quotation?

And the light was for all time, and the love was for all men.

Henry Clay supposedly said, "Statistics is no substitute for common sense." What was the context?

Where can one find the balance of this quotation, used by President Reagan in a brief speech at the All-Star Pre-Inaugural Gala aired on ABC? "For the pure pearls of tears, the gold of laughter, and the diamonds of stardust, they spread upon an otherwise dreary world."

He who does not advance loses count.

They paused to weep at Calvary and missed the Resurrection.

When the men of a nation will no longer fight that nation's wars, an enemy comes along, conquers that nation, and takes their women and breeds a better race of men.

Life is a chemical phenomenon.

I might know the chemical constituents of a cake down to the atomic weight of each component element; that fact would not help me to make a biscuit for a dog. Into its making many things enter: time, heat, pressure, etc.

Oh, the glory of the unspoken word!

Whenever I find myself in the presence of another human being, whatever his station, my dominant feeling is not so much to serve him or please him as not to offend his dignity.

Breasts are sex, but a leg is art.

In love's service only broken hearts qualify.

There is a peculiar tie that binds blood to blood which neither sin nor folly can sever.

A man absent is soon forgotten; a head on a gatepost is long remembered.

That is perfect, this is perfect, perfect comes from perfect. Take perfect from perfect and the remainder is perfect. Peace. Peace. Peace.

A touch of vulgarity adds charm to a woman.

When you come to the edge of all the light you have known, and you are about to step out into the darkness, Faith is knowing one of two things will happen. There will be something solid to stand on, or you will be taught how to fly.

Marshall McLuhan is supposed to have said, "In the nineteenth century schools knew more than the kids—in the twentieth century kids know more than the schools." What is the exact source for this?

What is the context of this quotation by Stephen Zweig: "What we call evil is the instability inherent in all mankind which drives man outside and beyond himself toward an unfathomable something."

Remain as uninhibited as the wild asses of the desert.

He went broke gradually and then suddenly.

He went mad singing in thirds.

Winston Churchill is supposed to have said, when asked why a bulldog has a pug nose, "so he can still breathe, without letting go." What is the exact source for this?

Be careful how you pick up the burden of hate, for it is a heavier load than you know.

Any man who thinks he understands women is a fool. Any man who truly understands women is immoral.

Oliver Wendell Holmes is supposed to have said, "What lies behind us and what lies before us are tiny matters compared to what lies within us." What is the true source for this?

It's all right to believe in evolution as long as you don't believe it happened by accident.

Watchman, how is it with the child?

Oh, how this world has changed.

To be born free is an accident, to live in freedom a responsibility, to die free—an obligation.

God plays the organ while the devil blows the bellows.

The greatest show on earth is a man talking.

Knowledge is the lamp that lights man's path to God.

We need a war every ten years to keep the population down.

Give then the raised right hand.

Death reigns, dust unto dust must go.

Husbands is the people your mommas marry.

We are not on the tennis court to see if the lines are straight, but to play tennis.

What I know I do not know for sure, but wherever I am ignorant, my ignorance is perfection.

Women faint and grown men shake with fear.

The engineer is a dreamer, a visionary; he dreams and dreams and dreams; he builds and builds and builds. Where the money is to come from he dreams and dreams and dreams.

Not what thou art, nor yet what thou has been, beholdeth God with his merciful eyes; but what thou wouldst be.

See that dog—he runs Athens. The dog runs the boy who runs the mother who runs the man who runs Athens.

Poem Fragments

Here are some fragments of poetry, very meaningful to some patron (and probably more than one somewhere), looking for a home with the rest of the poem. In most cases, if the title is unknown, the lines given probably represent either beginning or ending stanzas.

Sand / and Surf / and the Deep / and Distant Sea / and in the forest? A hermit's bell / Rebukes / and comforts me

"On the Cape," which begins, "We drove the Indians out of the land / But a dire revenge these redmen planned."

Four stanzas of four lines each on the theme of David, Bathsheba, and Uriah the Hittite.

"The Cold Bed Pan."

A poem that begins with these lines:

> Gaunt with the gray of the ages,
> Gnarled by the grip of time
> Glad when the wild wind rages
> Silent, secure, sublime.

A poem with the following lines:

> Mama hears her darling's prayer,
> tucks him safely into bed,
> Handies folded, peepers shut
> Nitegown white as white can be.

"Casey's Alibi": Remembered lines include:

> I'd been against that bloak before
> In addition, put him in the air.
> However, when the spitball butted in
> Well, Casey wasn't there.

"I wouldn't be a president, a king or duke, or earl / I'd rather be a dervish so I could whirl, and whirl, and whirl."

The poem titled "Hope" that begins "When all of life seems dark and dreary, keep on hoping."

The poem that includes these lines:

> Above far off in a lofty gloom,
> The words of a long dead people loom.
> Strange and savage and happy faced,
> and a curious mating of man and beast.

A poem reading: "and so I [offer] Melpomene this modest mead of praise / and crown my aging graying locks with Delphic oric lays."

"The burning logs give back the glow, of summer suns of long ago."

A poem by William Geiger titled "I Will Not Go Back."

What is the source of this prayer? "From the cowardice that shrinks from new truth."

"Far from affliction, toil, and care, the happy soul has fled."

"Grandpa has a wooden leg / he uses tacks for garters."

A poem with the following lines:

> Now Aliss Virginia Cleveland Brown,
> Since my Mama has gone to town,
> I'm going to give a lecture, dear.
> It's not a scolding, so don't you fear.
> The subject of it is going to be
> "Dolls invited out to tea."

"One Christmas Eve, an emigrant train."

"My life has grown rich with the passing of years."

"The Gray [or Grey] Engineer" by John Ink.

"The Ballad of the Supreme Court." It contains these lines:

> We're nine judicial gentlemen who shun the common herd.
> We're nine judicial mental men who speak the final word.
> We're nine judicial gentlemen above the storm and strife;
> Some president appoints us and we're put away for life.

An anonymous poem titled "Cynic's Prayer" which begins, "Thank you for the sky / Thank you for the grass" and ends "and if you don't exist, my gratitude is unchanged."

"Freedom's Plow."

President Reagan quoted a poem in a press conference. Lines quoted read:

> The bullfight critics ranked in rows
> Fill the enormous plaza full
> But there is only one who really knows
> and he's the one who fights the bull.

"What Ever Happened to Grandma?"

"I love you more than yesterday, but less than tomorrow."

In 1926, a husband quoted a poem in a love letter to his wife including these lines:

> In the house of calm affection
> In the house of social glee
> Should you ever think of any
> Would you kindly think of me.

"The Crowd Within."

"Outside my window, a new day I see / and only I can determine what kind of day it will be."

"If this be all, and when we die we die, then life is but a wanton, monstrous lie."

"Jimmy Jump Up," something recited by the patron's husband in the 1950s.

A patron learned a poem in school he would like to find. The only remembered lines are: "How glibly do they speak of war . . . and not a thing designed to kill."

"If you die I'll hug your grave." Supposedly it is part of a poem titled "Paths of Glory" by Robert or Richard Gray. It is not "Elegy Written in a Country Churchyard" by Thomas Gray.

A book of poems titled, *Thoughts of a Lonely Man and Other Poems* is supposedly authored by a poet connected to Harvard University with the middle name of Sumner. Who is this poet?

"Heights of Liningraf," which ends with the line, "to Liningraf."

"Where was I this time last night? I was high in a willow tree."

What about a poem about the hereafter?

> Will we know in the hereafter
> The things that now are hid?
> Does the butterfly remember
> What the caterpillar did?

"Sorrow not given vent in tears makes other organs weep."

"Take now the fruits of our labors / Nourish and guard them with care."

"He lost the game, no matter for that."

"Miracle of Weeds."

"Kelly's Dream." It begins:

> About a year ago I was invited
> By an old time friend of mine
> To come up to his residence
> To taste his beer and wine.

The final entry in the lost poem category:

> Out of your cage! Out of your cage!
> With rocks in your shoes if you must,
> But out of your cage, before you turn to dust.

People and Places

Stephen Vincent Benét's *American Names* includes a place named "Blind Man's Oast." An oast is a kiln for drying hops, malt, or tobacco, but where in the world is Blind Man's Oast?

R. L. Sharpe wrote a poem that is cited in *Granger's Index to Poetry,* sixth edition, and can be found in *Bartlett's Familiar Quotations,* thirteenth centennial edition, and *The Home Book of Quotations,* tenth edition. The poem appears under two titles, "Stumbling Block or Stepping-Stone" and "A Bag of Tools." Sharpe is an American author who flourished about 1890. The patron was looking for biographical information about Sharpe.

William de la Strange was a seaman who came to America in the service of Lafayette during the American Revolution. He also made cabinets for clocks, but the patron could not find any other print reference to this man.

Corrie Crandall Howell wrote a one-act play, *The Forfeit,* which appeared in *Poet Lore,* 36:136-41 (1925). However, no further biographical information, even at the Library of Congress, could be found.

Words and Phrases

From word play to peculiar expressions, "The Exchange" received a wide gamut of requests. The perennial, "What three words in the English language end in *gry*" has occupied many reference librarians over the years. In other cases, undefined words in books or half-remembered phrases send people to reference desks. Here are some nubbins of the English language that came to the column.

A World War I phrase—Gumshoe Jack

Why do people say, "You don't have to be a wizard out of Wales to know something like that"? This question was asked in 1970 and now, perhaps, has been replaced with, "You don't have to be a rocket scientist to figure that out."

Little Miss Rich Bitch

What is the word for a facility for spelling backward?

There is an expression that reads, "It'll take from now to juvember to finish all this work." When is juvember?

Western fans would like to know where the phrase "Scratch Gravel, White Wind" originated.

Why are "congo bars" called congo?

Edmund Gosse uses the word "chattafin" in the title of one of his poems. What does this word mean?

Miscellany

Finally, we end with a category of questions that simply does not fit easily in any of the earlier sections:

What is the history of clothes hangers?

Where did crepe paper originate?

What is the world's oldest river?

There is a code embedded in the closing credits of television serials. It consists of one or two letters, a hyphen, and three numbers (e.g., S-123). The code appears in the center of the last frame of the end credits, just above the line of trade associations. What does this code mean?

What is the most popular spectator sport in the world?

Can you sleep without dreaming?

What became of the Beth Israel Home, a settlement house for sick or indigent young women which existed in 1926 in New York City?

Where is there a single list for the official animals of countries?

In the 1950s there was a man who would testify at court cases involving DDT and, to prove the insecticide was harmless, would drink a DDT "cocktail." What happened to this man?

Where can I find a humorous piece that parallels Andy Griffith's "What It Was, Was Football" but deals with an outsider's interpretation of a traditional Latin Mass that pits the priest against two acolytes?

Where can I find a recipe for pin money pickles?

Who made the first designer blue jeans?

What college sport is played with the left hand only?

Why did Max Planck choose the letter "h" to represent Planck's constant?

Who wrote the music piece titled "When the Mist Covered the Mountain," which was played at the funeral of President Kennedy?

What is the origin of the song "Kum Ba Yah"?

Conclusion

If we are to make sense of where our profession is going, we need to at some point in time become a bit more proactive in thinking about the impact of the change the field is experiencing. For instance, assume for the moment there is at least some truth in the remark by Penniman to the effect that "Librarians are a curious enigma. Librarians have a long history of dealing with change, but in a schizophrenic way. They cling to the past, and yet they are often the heaviest users of technologies, such as computing and telecommunications resources" (Penniman, 1992). Given this, how does our inherent schizophrenia about technology limit our understanding and ability to make the most effective use of the nonlinear and rapidly changing world of Internet reference service? We embrace the greatly increased access to resources via the Internet and at the same time rail at the amount of misleading information, the difficulty of drilling down to relevant hits, and the lack of stability of URLs. It is easy to see how this love-hate relationship can work against a continuing involvement of the staff in using Web tools.

With our print-oriented, frozen-in-time emphasis on stability of information, we are having difficulties in dealing with the fluid nature of the Web. We even keep trying to force it into a print mold by attempts to "index" the contents. Interestingly enough, the public, lacking our rigorous training in source relevance and accuracy, often does not perceive this problem. Our users, at least those that are beginning to use the Web in our libraries, are often quite happy to do the electronic equivalent of hailing a passing stranger with a question. As librarians, this behavior concerns us because we know they are not getting the "best information," or "all the relevant information." It is inevitable that we share these concerns given the training and dedication that we have brought to reference librarianship as a profession. However, I am not sure how far into the new millennium we can hang on to this baggage—or at what point the constraints of linear reference will begin to impinge and limit how we can make the best use of new technological tools for helping our users understand the new world.

A paper posted on the Web by Bernie Sloan, GSLIS, University of Illinois at Urbana-Champaign titled, "Service Perspectives for the Digital Library" at <http://alexia.lis.uiuc.edu/~b-sloan/e-ref.html> sheds some light on possible developments. In addition to commenting on electronic reference service, Sloan cites another article by Clay Hathorn (1997), "The Librarian Is Dead, Long Live the Librarian." Hathorn suggests two possible models for reference in the future. In one scenario, a wealth of information is easily available to all and the librarian has become irrelevant. In the other scenario, there is a wealth of information, but it has become so difficult to access and interpret that the librarian is a central figure in mediating between data and user. The author suggests the future is somewhere between these two paradigms—certainly the safest kind of prediction to make!

Appendix

On the occasion of the twenty-fifth anniversary of the publication of *RQ*, each regular column in the Fall 1985 issue was preempted by a summary of the history of the column. In the case of "The Exchange," this summary was collectively developed by the Reference and Adult Services Division Bibliography Committee (RASD, 1985). What follows is an extract from the most pertinent parts of this summary.

Tricky questions, notes on unusual information sources, and general comments concerning reference problems and their solutions are wanted for "The Exchange." Since "The Exchange" column's inception in 1965, this quarterly call for contributions has gone out to the readers of *RQ*. "The Exchange" has become a printed vehicle through which librarians from all types of libraries have carried on a lively reference dialogue for over two decades in hopes of finding solutions to unanswered questions—the bane of the reference librarian's existence. In commemoration of the guidance, persistence, and good humor of the column's six editors, of the hundreds of librarians who mailed in the unsolved queries, and of the equal number of librarians who used their collective expertise and wisdom to provide clever, creative, and often whimsical answers, this silver anniversary article takes an anecdotal, personal, and slightly statistical look back on twenty-five years of "The Exchange."

History and Development of "The Exchange"

Over the past two decades, "The Exchange" has been guided by six different editors, each developing a distinct column personality and tone. The inaugural "Exchange" appeared in the winter 1965 issue of *RQ* under the tutelage of Thelma Freides. She introduced herself and the newly conceived column to *RQ* readers with the following opening paragraph:

> Every reference librarian has a private stock of bibliographic projects and discoveries worked out for his own use and consigned to memory or a filing cabinet as insufficiently elaborate or unique for publication. Yet information of value to one librarian is probably of use to others. Hence, with this issue *RQ* institutes "The Exchange" for unusual in-

formation source [*sic*], alternatives to "standard" sources when the latter are not available, questions for which a source could not be found, answers to the questions, and anything else which readers of *RQ* think might usefully be shared.

After three years of nurturing the column from an irregular contribution to a standard *RQ* feature, Freides passed on the pen in 1969 to the second editor, Mary Jo Lynch.

Mary Jo Lynch's term spanned 1969-1973, four years that helped to establish "The Exchange" as an *RQ* institution. Lynch remembers her work on the column with the fondness of a mother watching a child grow to adulthood. Since there was not always an overabundance of material, Lynch closed each issue with creative pleas for contributions that were always heard by her loyal and constant contributors. Nancy Gwinn directed and further shaped "The Exchange" from 1973 to 1976, reasserting Thelma Freides' original intent with this directive:

> Along with the queries and answers, however, I would also like to include in the column information about unusual reference sources, new methods of reference searching, interesting uses of local files or finding aids—in short, anything of value to your reference work which you would like to share with your fellow librarians.

Throughout her editorship, she presented responses in the framework of systematic approaches to reference work whenever possible, but she noted in her final column:

> Over the past two years that I have been editing this column, approximately 50 questions have been published, and over half of them received some kind of answer, either completely solving the problem or providing further clues or partial solutions. Some of the queries that I considered impossible were answered right away. In other cases, I found the same query popping up all over the country, with librarians everywhere contributing to the race for an answer.

When the fourth editor, David Berquam, took charge in 1976, "The Exchange" was indeed a healthy *RQ* institution averaging three to four pages an issue (a substantial increase from the early one-page columns). Berquam was open to any sort of question, letting the material contributed determine the philosophical direction of the column. He does, however, remember excluding one question because he felt the column would be better off without it. A reader wrote in requesting a list of publishers of pornography, and Berquam decided to let the matter be settled elsewhere. When he passed on the editorial reins in 1981 after an unprecedented five years, the column boasted a new, distinctive head and an international readership.

Gail Porter Bardhan, the column's fifth editor, compiled "The Exchange" from 1981 to 1984. In her editorial eyes, "The Exchange" continued to be a vehicle for communication among librarians seeking help on questions they could not solve, particularly quotation and word-source queries. In addition to the questions sent in by *RQ* readers, Bardhan scavenged questions from *Nexus,* a publication of the Systems Reference Service, North Suburban Library System, Wheeling, Illinois, and also received lists of teasers from the telephone reference service at Chicago Public Library.

Charles Anderson, the sixth and present editor, has only been at the helm for a short time, taking over the column in 1984. During this brief period, he has directed the column toward traditional reference questions and away from etymological explanations and quotation puzzles. [Note: This new direction did not long persist, perhaps because of the popularity of quotation questions as noted elsewhere in this summary.]

Column Contributors

While the six editors have provided the philosophical and organizational direction for the first twenty-five years of "The Exchange," the contributors have provided the questions and the answers—the heart of the column. While each editor might point to specific readers who repeatedly came through with sparkling witticisms or unusual approaches to reference, the column owes credit for its success to the large numbers and diversity of contributors.

Column Content

If "The Exchange" can be viewed as a forum for librarians who have exhausted their own reference expertise and available sources in pursuit of specific answers, then the column is highlighting problem areas for reference librarians as well as indicating needed reference sources. Since the beginning of "The Exchange," 345 questions have been published in the column, challenging librarians to apply their knowledge and professional skills. By examining the types of questions printed, the subject focus of the queries, the column's success rate, and the memorable puzzles, librarians can gain insight into problems posed in the delivery of reference service.

Type of Questions

Despite the inherent problems involved in categorizing types of reference questions, thirteen question types emerged when reviewing the first twenty-five years of "The Exchange." Each of the 345 queries was examined and placed into one of the thirteen categories to learn what types of questions cause reference librarians the most difficulty. The thirteen categories of question types include quotations, word or phrase origins, facts, bibliographic verifications, poem identifications, scientific or technical definitions, requests for a list, game and sport rules, requests for a source, customs, cultural or artistic definitions, symbols, and miscellaneous. For librarians who have tried unsuccessfully to track down a quotation's source after *Bartlett's* has failed, it will be no surprise that over 50 percent of all the questions posed in "The Exchange" have been concerned with quotes and word or phrase origins.

Subject Analysis of Questions

Subject analysis of the questions provides additional insight into the use of the column and the challenges presented to reference librarians. Using a general subject scheme that divides knowledge into the humanities, social sciences, and sciences, each query was assigned a specific subject area within one of these three divisions. Whenever possible, each question was classified in a specific category. However, fifty-six questions defied subject constraints, so a general category was added. The majority of the general queries were, not surprisingly, quotation problems. Examples of questions classified as "general" include the origin of the quote "curiosity killed the cat, satisfaction brought it back."

The subject analysis of the 345 questions points to the humanities as the dominant subject division represented. With over 62 percent of the questions concerned with the humanities, the commonly held notion of both availability of reference tools and quality of bibliographic control in the humanities seems suspect.

Success Rate

How successful has "The Exchange" been in answering the questions mailed in over the last twenty-five years? To determine the success rate of the column, each of the 345 questions submitted was tracked throughout the column's history to determine if a satisfactory answer ever was proposed. Regular readers of the column, concentrating on answers, probably do not realize that over 50 percent of the questions have not been resolved. Of the 345 questions posed in "The Exchange," 182 remain unsolved.

References

Preface

"The Exchange." (1985). *RQ*. Fall, 25:24-25.

Chapter 1

Albright, Peter, and Bets Parker Albright (1980). *Body, mind and spirit: The journey toward health and happiness*. Brattleboro, VT: Stephen Greene, pp. 16-17.

Bahn, Paul G. (1989). Early teething troubles. *Nature,* February 23, 337:693.

Bennett, Peter (1984). Tusk Scrubber a number one pick: Lowly, useful toothpick sails neatly through history. *Los Angeles Times,* December 14, 104:8.

Berkeley Fashions Inc. (1983). Telephone conversation with librarian.

Bok, Curtis (1959). *Star wormwood*. New York: Knopf, p. 228.

Brand, Oscar (1960). *Bawdy songs and backroom ballads*. New York: Dorcheser Press.

Brasch, Rudolph (1965). *How did it begin?* New York: D. McKay Co., pp. 22-23, 38.

Bremner, M.D.K. (1954). Mouth care through the ages. In *The story of dentistry*. Brooklyn, NY: Dental Items of Interest Publishing.

Brooke, Rupert (1935). Letter. *Golden Book Magazine,* January-June, p. 245.

Brooks, Gordon (1991). That old yellow ribbon. *Scan/Info.,* January, 3:1-2.

Brownmiller, Susan (1984). *Femininity*. New York: Linden Press/Simon & Schuster, p. 141.

Burchfield, R.W. (1978). Letter to the editor of "The Exchange."

Burrell, G.A. (1912). The use of mice and birds for detecting carbon monoxide after mine fires and explosions. U.S. Bureau of Mines Technical Paper, 11.

Caldwell, Jody (1989). Letter to the editor of "The Exchange."

Carter, Bill, and Carter, Joseph (1987). *Ethnodentristy and dental folklore*. Overland Park, KS: Dental Folklore Books of Kansas City.

Carter, Joseph (n.d.). *Of mice and tooth fairies*. n.p.

The Catholic Encyclopedia (1934). New York: Gilmary Society.

Chambers, R. (1967). *The book of days*. Detroit, MI: Gale Research Co., p. 568.

Champaign-Urbana News Gazette (1981). October 22, p. A-12.

Cirlot, Juan Eduardo. (1971). *A dictionary of symbols*. New York: Philosophical Library.

Note: In the earlier years of "The Exchange" the bibliographic citation control was not as rigorous as in later years. Consequently, some citations may be less than complete.

Coats, Alice M. (1971). *Flowers and their history*. New York: McGraw-Hill.

Cray, Edward (1962). Ethnic and place names as derisive adjectives. *Western Folklore,* January, pp. 21, 29+.

Dempsey, Donald (1962). Language of traffic policemen. *American Speech,* December, 37:267+.

Drury, Nevil (1992). *Dictionary of mysticism and the esoteric traditions*. San Francisco: Harper and Row.

The Economist (1991). March 2.

Encyclopedia Britannica Micropaedia (1976). Fifteenth Edition. Volume 5. Chicago: Encyclopedia Britannica.

Encyclopedia Judaica (1971). Volume 11. New York: The Macmillan Co.

Evening Tribune (1979). November 8.

Feldman, David (1986). *Imponderables: The solution to the mysteries of everyday life*. New York: Morrow, p. 29.

Geisey, Barbara (1987). Letter to the editor of "The Exchange."

Haldane, J. S., and C. G. Douglas (1909-1910). Testing for carbon monoxide in connection with fires and explosives in mines. In *Transactions/Institute of Mining Engineers,* pp. 38:267-80.

Hamer, Mick (1987). *New Scientist*. December 25, p. 16.

Hopper, Richard H. (1982). Left-right: Why driving rules differ. In *Transportation Quarterly,* October, 36:541-548.

The Hostess Book (1928). Milwaukee, WI: The Journal Company, p. 32.

Kanner, Leo (1928). *Folklore of the teeth*. New York: The Macmillan Co.

Lermontov, Mikhail Yurievich (1958). *A hero of our time*. Garden City, NY: Doubleday. Originally published 1840.

Los Angeles Times (1981). July 17.

_____. (1984). September 7, pt. 1-A, p. 3.

MacHaffied, Ingebord, and Margaret A. Nielsen (1976). *Of Danish way*. Minneapolis, MN: Dillon Press, p. 121.

Man, myth, and magic (1983). New York: Marshall Cavendish.

McCarthy, James Remington (1945). *Rings through the ages, an informal history*. New York: Harper and Brothers, pp. 154-157, 170-171, 176-177.

Merrill, Elmer Truesdell, ed. (1951). *Catullus works*. Cambridge, MA: Harvard University Press, pp. 39-40.

The New York Times (1980). November 5.

Opie, Iona, and Peter Opie (1959). *The lore and language of school children*. Oxford: Oxford University.

Peoples of the Earth (1973). Suffern, NY: Danbury Press.

Perica, Esther (1975). Letter to the editor of "The Exchange."

Phinney, Hart (1993). [Library Director at the Institute of Paper and Science Technology, Atlanta, GA.] Personal conversation with librarian.

Plumb, Beatrice, and Mabel N. Fuller (1951). *Wedding anniversary celebrations*. Minneapolis, MN: T. S. Denison and Co.

Proskauer, Curt (1946a). The care of the mouth in Greece and Rome. *CIBA Symposia,* November, 8:454-461.

_____. (1946b). Oral hygiene in the ancient and medieval orient. *CIBA Symposia,* November, 8:438-453.

Sales, Charles (Chic) (1929). *The specialist.* St. Louis, MO: Specialist Publishing, pp. 22-23.

SCAN (1978). Letter to the editor of "The Exchange."

Science News (1988). October 8, p. 237.

Sharper, Knowlson T. (1930). *Origins of popular superstitions and customs.* London: T. Werner Laurie, pp. 231-232.

Shepherd, Massey H. (1973). *Oxford American prayer book commentary.* New York: Harper, p. 302.

Sloan, Eric (1963). *A B C book of early Americana.* Garden City, NY: Doubleday and Co.

_____. (1967). *The cracker barrel.* New York: Funk and Wagnalls, p. 57.

Snyder, Henry L. (1949). *Our college colors.* Kutztown, PA: Kutztown Pub. Co., pp. 17-19.

Spaeth, Sigmund (1948). *History of popular music in America.* New York: Random House, pp. 83-84.

Spicer, Dorothy G. (1958). *Festivals of Western Europe.* New York: Wilson, p. 27.

Steinbeck, John (n.d.). *Travels with Charley.* New York: Viking, p. 189.

Stimpson, George (1948). *Information roundup.* New York: Harper & Brothers, pp. 263-264.

Surdez, G. (1937). Russian roulette. *Collier's,* January 30.

Tuleja, Tad (1987). *Curious customs.* New York: Stonesong Press Inc., p. 47.

Tyler, Karen (n.d.). *Something you always wanted to know about almost everything.* n.p.

Weeks, Walter Scott (1926). *Ventilation of mines.* New York: McGraw-Hill.

Wilford, John Noble (1989). But did they floss? *The New York Times,* March 7, 138:C1.

Wolhrabe, Raymond A., and Werner E. Krusch (1972). *The land and people of Denmark.* Philadelphia, PA: Lippincott.

Wormser, Richard Edward (1966). *The Yellowlegs.* Garden City, NY: Doubleday.

Chapter 3

The AA Grapevine (1950). January, p. 6.

Allen, Henry (1987). On being and phoning: If a call falls on deaf ears, is it still a call? *The Washington Post Magazine,* March 29, p. W11.

The Atlantic (1913). March, p. 354.

Banana Records (1972). National Lampoon, Blue Thumb LP Radio.

Barnhart, Clarence L., and others (1973). *The Barnhart dictionary of new English since 1963.* New York: Barnhart/Harper Row, p. 253.

Bartlett, John (1980). *Familiar quotations.* Fifteenth edition. Boston: Little, Brown.

Beckson, Karl, and Arthur Ganz (1975). *Literary terms*. New York: Farrar, p. 181.

Benét, William Rose (1948). *The reader's encylopedia*. Volume 4. New York: Thomas Y. Crowell Co.

Benham, W. Gurney (1907). *A book of quotations, proverbs and household words*. Philadelphia, PA: J. B. Lippincott Co., p. 786.

Berkeley, George (1963). *The principles of human knowledge and three dialogues between Hylas and Philonous*. New York: Meridian Books, p. 162.

Berquam, David (1990). Letter to the editor of "The Exchange."

Bliss, Alan Joseph (1966). *Dictionary of foreign words and phrases in current English*. New York: Dutton, p. 181.

Bullock, Alan, and Oliver Stallybrass, eds. (1977). *The Harper dictionary of modern thought*. New York: Harper.

Caen, Herb (1975). *New York Times,* September 26, p. 37.

Carr, Edward H. (1958). *Socialism in one country*. New York: Macmillan, p. 148.

Cincinnatus (1980). *Self-destruction: The disintegration and decay of the U.S. army during the Vietnam era*. New York: Norton.

De Bono, Edward (1970). *Lateral thinking: Creativity step by step*. New York: Harper.

Demeyer, R.M. (1974). Letter to the editor of "The Exchange."

Dictionary of National Biography (1921). "James I of Scotland." London: Oxford University Press.

Dunker, Christoph, ed. (1973). *Ausblick von der Weibertereu; Kirchen im Bezirk Weinsberg*. Weinsberg: Röck.

Emerson, Ralph Waldo (1968). *Essays and journals*. Garden City, NY: International Collectors Library, p. 642.

Evans, Bergen (1969). *Dictionary of quotations*. New York: Delacorte, p. 569.

Facts on File encyclopedia of word and phrase origins (1987). New York: Facts on File, p. 15.

Fadiman, Clifton (1955). *The American treasury, 1455-1955*. New York: Harper, p. 984.

Flexner, Stuart Berg (1982). *Listening to America*. New York: Simon & Schuster, p. 500.

Fox, Paul (1992). *Thriving in tough times*. Hawthorne, NJ: Career Press, p. 47.

Gross, Leonard (1983). *How much is too much? The effects of social drinking*. New York: Random House, pp. 23-24.

Gunn, Lewis (1986). Letter to the editor of "The Exchange."

Hoffman, Abbie (1968). *Revolution for the hell of it*. New York: Dial Press.

Hubbard, Elbert (1913). *Complete writings*. Volume 17. East Aurora, NY: Roycroft, p. 243.

Humphrey, Hubert (n.d.). [From a 1964 speech quoted in *The Quote . . . Unquote Newsletter*.]

Joly, Henri L. (1967). *Legend in Japanese art*. Rutland, NY: Tuttle.

Larsen, Dave (1984). This telephone exhibition is a bell ringer. *Los Angeles Times,* January 4, pt. 5, p. 1.

Lean, Vincent Stuckey (1903). *Lean's Collectanea*. London: Arrowsmith.

Long Lines Magazine (1967). June.

Lynch, Mary Jo (1973). "The Exchange." *RQ*, Summer, p. 392.

Macmillan dictionary of quotations (1989). New York: Macmillan, p. 55.

Mariani, John F. (1999). *Encyclopedia of American food and drink*. New York: Lebhar-Friedman Books.

Morris, William, and Mary Morris (1988). *Dictionary of word and phrase origins*. New York: Harper.

Neaman, Judith S., and Carole G. Silver (1983). *Kind words: A thesaurus of euphemisms*. New York: Facts on File Publications, pp. 151-152.

The New York Times (1980). December 8, p. C-8.

Niebuhr, Ursula L. (1978). Letter to South Bay Area Reference Network.

Notes and queries (1970). June, 8:154.

The Oxford dictionary of quotations (1979). London: Oxford University Press, p. 72.

Oxford English dictionary (1989). Second edition. Oxford: Clarendon Press.

Partridge, Eric (1978). *Dictionary of the underworld*. Third edition. New York: Macmillan.

Pearce, Helen (1946). Folk sayings in a pioneer family of western Oregon. *California Folklore Quarterly*, Volume 5. July.

Pittsburgh Post-Gazette (1993). February, p. H1.

Plutarch (1979). *Lives of the noble Grecians and Romans*. New York: Modern Library.

Ramage, C.T. (n.d.). *Familiar quotations from Latin authors*. London: George Routledge and Sons, p. 466.

Rees, Nigel (n.d.). *The Quote . . . Unquote Newsletter*.

Safire, William (1972). *The new language of politics*. Don Mills, Ont., Canada: Collier, p. 337.

_____. (1978). *Political dictionary*. New York: Random House, pp. 18-19.

_____. (1980). *The New York Times Magazine* April 6, p. 10.

_____. (1982). Nine yards to hell. *The New York Times Magazine*, October 3, p. 12.

_____. (1990). *Fumblerules: A lighthearted guide to grammar and good usage*. New York: Doubleday.

Simpson, J.A. (1982). *The concise Oxford dictionary of proverbs*. New York: Oxford University Press, p. 13.

Stevenson, Burton (1959). *Home book of proverbs, maxims and familiar phrases*. New York: Dodd, p. 2611.

_____. (1967). *Home book of quotations*. New York: Dodd, p. 2611.

Time (1953). September 28, p. 22.

Tripp, R.T. (1970). *International thesaurus of quotations*. New York: Crowell.

Trotsky, Leon (1932). *The history of the Russian revolution*. Volume 3. New York: Simon & Schuster, p. 311.

Union Theological Seminary (1978). Letter to the editor of "The Exchange," including postcard from Niebuhr.

Walker, Joan, and Morton Walker (1973). *Think and grow thin.* New York: Arco, p. 114.

Watson, Lillian Eichler (1951). *Light from many lamps.* New York: Simon & Schuster.

Wilson, Logan (1942). *The academic man: A study in the sociology of a profession.* New York: Oxford University Press, p. 147.

Winn, Godfrey (1963). *Daily Sketch,* October 7.

Chapter 4

Anderson, Charles R. (2001). Reference librarianship: A guide for the 21st century. In Celia Hales Mabry, ed., *Doing the work of reference.* Binghamton, NY: The Haworth Information Press, pp. 5-19.

Chapter 5

The American Cemetery (1938). Successful cemetery advertising. March, p. 13.

American Poetry Review (1975), pp. 23-26.

Arion (1969). 8:461-464.

Arnheim, Rudolph (1948). *Poets at work: Essays based on the modern poetry collection at the Lockwood Memorial Library, University of Buffalo.* New York: Harcourt, Brace.

Bartlett, John (1980). *Familiar quotations.* Fifteenth edition. Boston, MA: Little, Brown.

Beatty, Jerome (1960). Trade winds. *Saturday Review,* December 20.

Benham, Sir Gurney (1924). *Benham's book of quotations, proverbs, and household words.* New York: Putnam, p. 751a.

Boller, Paul F. Jr., and John George (1989). *They never said it.* New York: Barnes and Noble Books, pp. 45-46.

Byrnes, Robert (1982). *The 637 best things anybody ever said.* New York: Atheneum.

Campbell, Harry, and Kenneth Campbell, eds. (1936). *Aids to pathology.* London: Baillière, Tindall & Cox.

Cappon, Lester J., ed. (1988). *The Adams-Jefferson letters.* Chapel Hill, NC: University of North Carolina.

Carpenter, Francis (1866). *Six months at the White House.* New York: Hurd and Houghton, pp. 258-259.

Carroll, Lewis (1970). *Alice's adventures in wonderland and through the looking glass.* Racine, WI: Whitman.

Clark, Ramsey (1968). *Proceedings of the Ninety-Seventh Annual Congress of Correction.* Washington, DC: American Correctional Association, p. 4.

Craik, Dinah Maria Mulock (1903). *A life for a life.* London: Harper & Brothers, p. 84.

cummings, e.e. (1965). *e. e. cummings: A miscellany.* Revised edition with an introduction and notes by George J. Firmage. New York: October House, p. 335.

Darrah, L.W. (1939). The difficulty of being normal. *Journal of Nervous and Mental Disorder,* 90:6.

Day, Clarence (1920). *The story of the Yale University Press told by a friend.* New Haven, CT: Yale University Press.

Dictionary of American Biography (1928-1937). New York: Scribner's.

Durant, Will (1926). *The story of philosophy.* New York: Simon & Schuster, p. 241.

Esar, Evan (1978). *The comic encyclopedia.* Garden City, NY: Doubleday, p. 54.

Finnegan, Greg (1991). Letter to the editor of "The Exchange."

Ford, Gerald (1974). *Public papers of the presidents.* Washington, DC: Government Printing Office, p. 103.

Frisch, Sylvia (1990). Letter to the editor of "The Exchange," reporting on a NEXIS search.

Genner, Ernest Ely, ed. (1928). *Selections from the Attic orators.* Oxford: The Clarendon Press.

Green, Jonathon, ed. (1982). *Morrow's international dictionary of contemporary quotations.* New York: Morrow, p. 49.

Harnsberger, Caroline Thomas (1950). *The Lincoln treasury.* Chicago: Wilcox and Follet Co., p. 275.

Hays, Gilbert (1979). *Golden harvest.* New York: Doubleday, p. 3.

Herman, Judy (1986). Letter to the editor of "The Exchange."

Hesiod (1959). *Works and days.* Ann Arbor, MI: University of Michigan Press, lines 289-291.

Holcomb, Laurel (1970). Letter to the editor of "The Exchange."

Hoover, Herbert (1963). *Fishing for fun and to wash your soul.* New York: Random House.

Hoyt's new cyclopedia of practical quotations (1940). New York: Grosset & Dunlap.

Humphrey, Hubert H. (1977). Remarks at the dedication of the Hubert H. Humphrey HEW Building, November 1, 1977. *Congressional Record,* November 4, 123: 37287.

Hyde, F. Montgomery (1973). *Baldwin: The unexpected prime minister.* London: Hart-David.

Jeffersonian cyclopedia (1900). Volume 2. New York: Funk & Wagnalls.

Kaiser, Rudolph (1987). Chief Seattle's speeches: American origins and European reception. In Brian Swann and Arnold Krupat, eds., *Recovering the word: Essay on Native American literature.* Berkeley, CA: University of California Press, pp. 497-536.

Keller, Robert (1990). Haida Indian land claims and South Moresby National Park. *American Review of Canadian Studies,* Spring, p. 7.

Kerber, August (1968). *Quotable quotes in education.* Detroit, MI: Wayne State University Press, p. 2.

Keyes, Ralph (1992). *Nice guys finish seventh*. New York: HarperCollins.

Larkin, Oliver W. (1949). *Art and life in America*. New York: Rinehart and Co., p. 229.

Law, William (1986). *Christian perfection*. Wheaton, IL: Tyndale House.

Lewis, C.S. (1954). *English literature in the sixteenth century excluding drama*. Oxford: Clarendon Press, p. 58.

London, Joan (1968). *Jack London and his times*. New York: Doubleday, Doran, reprinted by the University of Washington Press, p. 372.

Los Angeles Times (1985). August 21, pt. 5, p. 1.

Los Angeles Times Calendar (1986). March 30, p. 79.

MacDonell, Sir John (1983). *Historical trials* [facsimile edition]. Littleton, CO: F. B. Rothman, p. 148.

Maugham, Somerset (1943). *W. Somerset Maugham's introduction to modern English and American literature*. Philadelphia, PA: The Blakiston Company, p. 350.

Mencken, H.L. (1942). *A new dictionary of quotations*. New York: Knopf.

Morley, John (1901). *Voltaire: A contemporary vision*. New York: DuMont, p. 228.

Mossé-Bastide, R.M., comp. (1957). *Henri Bergson: Écrits et paroles*. Paris: Presses Universitaires de France, p. 649.

Motley, Willard (1947). *Knock on any door*. New York: Appleton-Century-Crofts Co.

The New York Times Book Review (1971). June 27.

Nouvelles littéraires (1937). September 11.

O'Meara, Barry (1822). *Napoleon in exile; or, a voice from St. Helena*. Volume 2. Philadelphia. PA: Carey and Lea, p. 44.

Oxford English Dictionary (OED) (1989). Oxford: Clarendon Press.

Payne, Robert (1950). *Mao Tse-tung, ruler of Red China*. New York: Henry Schuman, p. 275.

Perry, Ted (1970). *Home* [film].

Phillips, Charles (1817). *The Speeches of Charles Phillips, Esq*. London: Longman, Hurst, Reese, Orme, and Brown.

Platt, Suzy (1993). *Respectfully quoted*. Washington, DC: Library of Congress.

Pyarelal (1959). *Towards new horizons*. Ahmedabad: Navajivan Publishing House.

Radford, Neil A. (1978). Letter to the editor of "The Exchange."

Richard, Paul (1929). *The scourge of Christ*. New York: Knopf.

Running Press Staff, eds. (1989). *Quotable women: A collection of shared thoughts*. Philadelphia, PA: Running Press.

Sa'di, Muslin-ed-Din (1865). *The Gulistan or rose garden*. Translated by Francis Gladwin. Boston, MA: Ticknor & Fields.

Safire, William (1980). The triumph of evil. *The New York Times,* March 9, 6:8+.

Saltus, Edgar (1917). *Oscar Wilde*. Chicago: Brothers of the Book.

San Francisco Examiner (1952). November 11.

Santayana, George (1905). *The life of reason,* Volume 1. New York: C. Scribner's Sons.

Schumacher, E. F. (1999). *Small is beautiful.* Vancouver, BC: Hartley & Marks Publishers, p. 20.

Shelley, Percy Bysshe (1812). *Proposals for an association.* February 12.

Shipps, Anthony (1976). Reply. *Notes and queries NS,* July 23, 312.

_____. (1990). *The quote sleuth; A manual for the tracer of lost quotations.* Urbana and Chicago: University of Illinois Press.

Smith, Henry A. (1887). *Seattle Sunday Star,* October 29.

Snow, Helen F. (1939). *Inside Red China.* New York: Doubleday, p. vii.

Spear, Hilda D., ed. (1974). *The English poems of Charles Stuart Calverley.* Leicester: Leicester University Press, p. 37.

Stanley, Bessie A. (1911). What is success? In *Heart Throbs,* Volume 2. Boston, MA: Chapple.

Stevenson, Burton (1934). *The home book of quotations, classical and modern.* New York: Dodd, Mead.

Stone, Peter (1970). *1776: A musical play.* New York: The Viking Press.

Taylor, Arche, and Bartlett Whiting, eds. (1958). *Dictionary of American proverbs and proverbial phrases, 1820-1880.* Cambridge, MA: Harvard University Press, p. 233.

Tindall, Elizabeth (1978). Letter to the editor of "The Exchange."

Tripp, Rhoda Thomas (1970). *International thesaurus of quotations.* New York: Thomas Y. Crowell, p. 219.

United States President (1969-1974: Nixon). *Richard Nixon, containing the public speeches, messages, and statements of the President.* Washington, DC: Government Printing Office, 1971-1974.

The universal songster, or museum of mirth London (1828). London: Jones and Co., p. 143.

Usher, Elizabeth (1967). Inaugural speech. *Special Libraries,* August.

Wilde, Oscar (1946). *The portable Oscar Wilde.* New York: Viking Press, p. 660.

Chapter 6

Ferrell, J.E. (1990). Saving clean air from its last gasp. *Chicago Tribune,* May 27.

Plaiss, Mark (1985). Stupid reference questions. *Library Journal,* October 15, 110:46.

Platt, Suzy (1993). *Respectfully quoted.* Washington, DC: Library of Congress.

Chapter 7

Adler, Ron (1974). *Looking out/looking in: Interpersonal communications.* San Francisco: Rinehart Press.

Adshead, Gladys L., and Annis Duff (1948). *An inheritance of poetry*. Boston, MA: Houghton.

Arbuthnot, May Hill, and Sheldon L. Root Jr. (1968). *Time for poetry,* Third edition. Glenview, IL: Scott, Foresman and Co., p. 116.

Auden, W.H. (1966). *Collected shorter poems, 1927-1957*. New York: Random House.

Best, Dick, and Beth Best (1967). *Song fest*. New York: Crown, p. 131.

Blatchford, Court (1984). Mary Frye's poetry wins national acclaim—50 years later. *Dundalk Eagle,* August 8.

Blietz, Cynthia S. (1982). Letter to the editor of "The Exchange."

Bouton, Josephine (1962). *Poems for the children's hour*. New York: Platt & Munk.

Bunner, H.C. (1897). *The poems of H.C. Bunner*. New York: Scribner.

Chicago Tribune (1976). September 16, section 1, p. 5.

Cole, William (1959). *The fireside book of humorous poetry*. New York: Simon & Schuster, p. 342.

Coward, Noël (1943). *Don't let's be beastly to the Germans/The welcoming land,* recitation written by Clemence Dane. HMV B9336.

Daly, T.A. (1912). *Madrigali*. Philadelphia, PA: David McKay, pp. 91-93.

Dana, Charles A. (1970). *The household book of poetry*. Freeport, NY: Books for Libraries Press, pp. 416-417.

Darrow, Clarence (1957). *The story of my life*. New York: Grosset and Dunlap.

Denver, John (1971). *Poems, prayers and promises*. RCA AYL1-5189.

Drenowatz, Margaret C. (1975). Letter to the editor of "The Exchange."

Emerson, Ralph Waldo, ed. (1875). *Parnassus*. Boston, MA: Osgood, p. 328.

The explicator cyclopedia (1966). Volume 2. Chicago: Quadrangle Books, pp. 10-14.

Felleman, Hazel (1936). *Best loved poems of the American people*. Garden City, NY: Garden City Publishing.

_____. (1965). *Poems that live forever*. Garden City, NY: Doubleday.

Fry, Caroline (1822). *Serious poetry*. London: Ogle, Duncan, and Co., pp. 102-106.

Gardner, Martin (1967). *The associated Casey at the bat*. New York: Clarkson N. Potter.

Gosik, Pamela (1996). Letter to the editor of "The Exchange."

Hardendorff, Jeanne B. (1974). *Sing song scuppernong*. New York: Holt, Rinehart and Winston.

Hay, Peter (1989). *The book of legal anecdotes*. New York: Facts on File, p. 112.

Herman, Judith (1993). Letter to the editor of "The Exchange."

Hill, Ralph Nading (1949). *The Winooski: Heartway of Vermont*. New York: Rinehart.

Housman, A.E. (1945). *The collected poems of A. E. Housman*. New York: Henry Holt and Co., p. 185.

Jackson, Joseph H., ed. (1952). *The western gate: A San Francisco reader*. New York: Farrar, Straus & Young, p. 441.

Kayes, Mary Jane (1977). Letter to the editor of "The Exchange."

Kennedy, Charles O'Brien (1952). *American ballads: Naughty, ribald and classic.* New York: Fawcett.

Kent, David (1992). *Forty whacks: New evidence in the life and legend of Lizzie Borden.* Emmaus, PA: Yankee, p. 206.

Kincaid, Bradley. *Ain't we crazy.* Bullet Record 615-A.

Lascelles, Kendrew (1974). *The Box.* Los Angeles: Nash Publishing Co.

Lederer, Richard (1994). *Adventures of a verbivore.* New York: Pocket Books, p. 36.

Library of the World's Best Literature (1896). Volume 15. New York: J.S. Peale and J.A. Hill, p. 8544.

Little Corporal (1872). Volume 14. January-June.

Lowell, James Russell (1925). *The complete poetical works of James Russell Lowell.* Boston: Houghton Mifflin.

Marshall, Michael (1979). *The Stanley Holloway monologues.* London: Elm Tree Books, pp. 29-32.

_____. (1981). *The book of comic and dramatic monologues.* London: Elm Tree Books, pp. 62-63.

Martin, Edward Sandford (1914). *Pomes.* New York: Scribner.

McColl, Ewan (n.d.). *Bad lads and hard cases.* Riverside Records RLP 12-632.

McNamara, M. Frances (1967). *2,000 famous legal quotations.* Rochester, NY: Aqueduct Books, p. 453.

Nash, Ogden (1957). *You can't get there from here.* Boston, MA: Little, Brown, pp. 32-33.

Nelson, Muriel (1979). Letter to the editor of "The Exchange."

New Adventist Hymnal (1952). Grantham, Lincolnshire (England): Stanborough Press.

New Oxford book of English verse (1972). New York: Oxford University Press.

"Non-persona. . . persona." (1973). *American Journal of Nursing,* June, p. 998.

Notes and queries (1955). December, 200:547.

O'Lachlainn, Colm (1960). *Irish street ballads.* No. 6. New York: Citadel Press.

Poems teachers ask for: Book One (1925). Danville, NY: F. A. Owen Pub.

Ragbag of legal quotations (1960). New York: Matthew Bender and Co., p. 222.

Rhymes of the playground (n.d.). p. 106. [The photocopied extract supplied as an answer had no additional bibliographic information. The closest reference located was Cynthia Mitchell's *Hop along happily, and other rhymes for the playground.* London: Heinemann, 1979. Given the pagination in the latter, this may not be the same as the cited work.]

Rowswell, Albert Kennedy (n.d.). *Aunt Minnie's scrapbook: Humorous tales of the diamond.* Sharpsburg, PA: Fort Pitt Brewing Company.

Russell, Ronald (1975). Lessons from life. In *Reader's Digest treasury of modern quotations.* New York: Reader's Digest Press.

Scheetz, George H. (1988). Letter to the editor of "The Exchange," February 26.

Senghas, Dorothy (1976). Letter to the editor of "The Exchange."

Seventh-Day Adventist encyclopedia (1976). Washington, DC: Review and Herald Publishing Association, p. 142.

Smith, Charlotte (1807). *Beachy Head: With other poems.* London: J. Johnson.

Spaeth, Sigmund (1927). *Weep some more, my lady.* New York: Doubleday.

Spiering, Frank (1984). *Lizzie.* New York: Random House, p. 203.

Stallworthy, Jon (1978). *A familiar tree.* New York: Oxford University Press.

Stevenson, Burton (1953). *The home book of verse,* vol. 1. New York: Holt.

Sting (1985). *The dream of the blue turtles.* A & M Records, SP-3750.

Stone, Irving (1941). *Clarence Darrow for the defense.* Garden City, NY: Doubleday, p. 417.

Swift, Jonathan (1958). *The poems of Jonathan Swift.* Second edition. Volume 2. Oxford: Clarendon Press, p. 651. (Originally published 1773)

Tolkien, J.R.R. (1966). *The Tolkien reader.* New York: Ballantine Books.

Van Waters, George. (1863). *The poetical geography.* New York: C. S. Westcott & Co.

Watson, Roy W. (1986). *Poetry worth remembering.* Lawrenceville, VA: Brunswick, p. 188.

Werner, E.S. (1906-1907). *Werner's readings and recitations.* New York: Edgar S. Werner, No. 37, pp. 107-108; No. 39, pp. 166-167; No. 54, pp. 168-169.

White, E.B. (1941). *Subtreasury of American humor.* New York: Coward-McCann Inc., pp. 704-705.

Williamson, Ruth (1979). [Curator of Riley Home in Greenfield, Indiana], personal correspondence to Amy Kellerstrass, Illinois State Library.

Chapter 8

Walker, Leslie (1996). On the Web, a catalogue of complexity. *The Washington Post,* November 25, p. F17.

Chapter 9

Adler, Bill (1966). *The Stevenson wit.* Garden City, NY: Doubleday & Co., p. 73.

Albertson, Christopher (1980). Letter to the editor of "The Exchange."

Alexander, Irene (1986). His art quickens the spirit. *Monterey Peninsula Herald.* May 14.

Blockson, Charles (1977). *Black genealogy.* Englewood Cliffs, NJ: Prentice-Hall, pp. 120-121.

Cassidy, Frederic G., ed. (1985). *Dictionary of American regional English,* Volume 1. Cambridge, MA: Belknap Press of Harvard University Press, p. 259.

Christopher, Maurice (1976). *Black Americans in Congress.* New York: Crowell.

Coffin, Tristram Potter, ed. (1968). *Our literary traditions.* New York: Basic Books, pp. 156-157.

Contemporary literary criticism (1973). Volume 1. Detroit, MI: Gale Research Co.
_____. (1984). Volume 29. New York: Gale Research Co.

Current Biography Yearbook 1975 (1975). New York: Wilson.

Darrow, Clarence (1957). *The story of my life.* New York: Grosset and Dunlap.

Denison, Paul (1982). *The Monterey Peninsula Herald Weekend Magazine.* November 7.

Dorson, Richard M. (1959). *American folklore.* Chicago: University of Chicago Press, pp. 124-128.

Downeast Magazine (1978). October, p. 27.

Ekwall, Eilert (1960). *The Concise Oxford dictionary of English place-names.* Oxford: Clarendon Press, pp. 18-19.

Foner, Philip S., ed. (1969). *The autobiographies of the Haymarket martyrs.* New York: Humanities Press, p. 59.

Du Bois, Shirley Graham, and George D. Lipscomb (1974). *Dr. George Washington Carver: Scientist.* New York: Julian Messner, pp. 230-231.

Gray, Jeffrey A. (1979). *Ivan Pavlov.* New York: Viking, p. 104.

Hollingshead, A.B. (1949). *Elmtown's youth.* New York: Wiley.

Holt, Rackham (1963). *George Washington Carver.* Garden City, NY: Doubleday.

Ireland, Tom (1942). *Ireland, past and present.* New York: Putnam, p. 126.

King, Seth (1984). *The New York Times,* October 16, p. 26.

Larousse encyclopedia of mythology (1959). New York: Prometheus Press.

Leedskalnin, Edward (1936). *A book in every home.* Homestead, FL: Leedskalnin.

Leonard, Owen L., and C.P. Loomis (1941). *Culture of a contemporary rural community.* Washington, DC: Bureau of Agricultural Economics.

Lexicon universal encyclopedia (n.d.). New York: Lexicon Publications Inc.

Lincoln, William Ensign (1930). *Some descendants of Stephen Lincoln of Wymondham, England; Edward Larkin from England, etc.* New York: Knickerbocker Press, p. 119.

The New York Times (1927). March 12.

The New York Times Book Review (1983). August 17, p. 23.

_____. (1984). October 16, p. 26.

Oxford English Dictionary Supplement (1982). Volume II. Oxford: Clarendon Press, p. 366.

Papineau, Anne (1984). *The Carmel Pine Cone/CV Outlook.* June 7, p. 25.

Portland Sunday Telegram (1959). July 5.

Robinson, Ronald, and J. Gallagher (1961). *Africa and the Victorians.* New York: St. Martin's, pp. 189-185.

Seely, John R., Alexander R. Sim, and Elizabeth W. Loosley (1956). *Crestwood Heights: A study of the culture of suburban life.* New York: Wiley.

Skermetta, Peter (1976). Letter to the editor of "The Exchange," *RQ,* Summer, 15:331.

Sunday Telegraph (London). (1983). January 23.

Taylor, Isaac (1898). *Names and their histories.* London: Rivingtons, p. 55.

Twentieth century crime and mystery writers (1980). New York: St. Martin's, p. 1392.

Vidich, Arthur J., and Joseph Bensman (1958). *Small town in mass society: Class, power and religion in a rural community.* Princeton, NJ: Princeton University Press, 1958.

West, James [pseud.] (1945). *Plainville, U. S. A.* New York: Columbia University Press, p. xv.

Chapter 11

Ars quatuor coronatorum (1969). Margate, England, 82:337.

Bunner, Kimberly (1992). Letter to author. April 9.

Bell, Leland V. (1980). *Treating the mentally ill from colonial times to the present.* New York: Praeger Publishers, p. 60.

Benét, William Rose (1987). *Benét's reader's encyclopedia.* Third edition. New York: Harper & Row, pp. 234, 874.

Biggar, H.P. (1924). *The Voyages of Jacques Cartier.* Ottawa, ON: F.A. Acland, Printer to the King's Most Excellent Majesty.

Bowyer, Jack (1977). *The evolution of church building.* New York: Whitney Library of Design.

Braun, Hugh (1971). *English abbeys.* London: Faber and Faber, p. 102.

_____. (1972). *Cathedral architecture.* New York: Crane and Russak.

Breeden, James O., ed. (1980). *Advice among masters: The ideal in slave management.* Westport, CT: Greenwood Press, pp. 172-174.

Brewer, Ebenezer Cobham (1970). *Brewer's dictionary of phrase and fable.* New York: Harper & Row.

Cook, George Henry (1954). *The English mediaeval parish church.* London: Phoenix House.

Davis, Herbert (1965). *The drapier's letters.* Oxford: Oxford University Press, p. 60.

Dekker, Thomas (1973). *The Belman of London.* New York: Da Capo Press, pp. 528, 530, 531.

Dickson, Paul (1982). *Dickson's word treasury: A connoisseur's collection of old and new, weird and wonderful, useful and outlandish words.* New York: Delacorte Press, p. 328.

Dixon, Eustace A. (1988). *Syndromes for the layperson: Now I know what's wrong with me.* Mantua, NJ: Eureka Publications.

Dvorak, John C. (1987). Origins of the word "nerd." *PC Magazine,* May 26, p. 91.

Flexner, Stuart Berg (1982). *Listening to America.* New York: Simon & Schuster, p. 477.

Funk, Charles Earle (1958). *Horsefeathers and other curious words.* New York: Harper.

_____. (1975). Letter to the editor of "The Exchange."

Geisel, Theodore Seuss (1950). *If I ran the zoo.* New York: Random House.

Gold, Robert S. (1975). *Jazz talk.* Indianapolis: Bobbs-Merrill, pp. 4-5.

Greene, Robert (1966). *The second part of conny-catching*. New York: Barnes and Noble, pp. 16-19.

Guiness book of world records (1988). London: Guiness World Records.

Hale, Judson, ed. (1991). *The best of the old farmer's almanac*. New York: Random House, p. 126.

The Harlem Renaissance (2001). Comp. Karen Kuehner. Evanston, IL: Nextext.

Harvey, Paul (1937). *The Oxford companion to classical literature*. Oxford: Clarendon Press, p. 162.

Hendrickson, Robert (1987). *The Henry Holt encyclopedia of word and phrase origins*. New York: Henry Holt and Co., pp. 85-86.

Hodge, Frederick Webb (1979). *Handbook of American Indians north of Mexico*. Totowa, NJ: Rowman and Littlefield, p. 705.

Hoyt's new cyclopedia of practical quotations (1940). New York: Grosset & Dunlap, pp. 85-86.

Larson, Jay (1992). Letter to author, April 6.

Lederer, Richard (1989). *Crazy English: The ultimate joy ride through our language*. New York: Pocket Books, pp. 74-75.

Lehnert, Martin (1971). *Rückläufiges wörterbuch der Englischen gegenwartssprache*. Leipzig: Verlag Enzyklopädie.

MacCulloch, John Arnott (1932). *The mythology of all races*. Index, Volume 13. Boston, MA: Marshall Jones Co., p. 48.

Major, Clarence (1970). *Dictionary of Afro-American slang*. New York: International Publishers.

Martin, Michael R., and Richard C. Harrier (1971). *The concise encyclopedic guide to Shakespeare*. New York: Horizon, pp. 20, 114.

Mays, David (1967). *The letters and papers of Edmund Pendleton II*. Charlottesville, VA: University Press of Virginia, for the Virginia Historical Society, pp. 387-388.

Moore, Linda (1995). Letter to the editor of "The Exchange."

Morris, William, and Mary Morris (1977). *Morris dictionary of word and phrase origins*. New York: Harper, p. 546.

Moskow, Shirley (1987). *Hunan hand*. Boston, MA: Little, Brown.

Oxford English Dictionary (1989). Revised second edition. Oxford: Oxford University Press.

Oxford English Dictionary Supplement (1982). Volume III. Oxford: Clarendon Press, p. 238.

Parker, James F. (1984). *The official price guide to collector's knives*. Seventh edition. Orlando, FL: House of Collectibles, p. 27.

Partridge, Eric (1984). *A dictionary of slang and unconventional English*. New York: Macmillan, p. 1459.

Pate, Jim (1988). Letter to the editor of "The Exchange."

Poulter, John (1779). *The discoveries of John Poulter, alias Baxter*. Sixteenth edition. London: R. Goadby & Co., p. 60.

Prentice, Sartell (1934). *The heritage of the cathedral*. New York: Morrow.

Raffe, W.G. (1964). *Dictionary of the dance*. New York: Barnes.

Random House dictionary of the English language (1966). New York: Random House.

Robinson, L.J. (1972). *A dictionary of graphical symbols*. London: F.C. Avis, p. 680.

Safire, William (1980). *On language*. New York: Times Books, p. 65.

Smithsonian Catalog (1988). Spring, p. 18.

Updike, Daniel Berkeley (1927). *Printing types: Their history, forms, and use.* Cambridge, MA: Harvard University Press, p. 18.

Urdang, Lawrence, ed. (1986).—*Ologies and —isms*. Third edition. Detroit, Gale, p. 171.

Weller, Charles (1918). *The early history of the typewriter*. La Porte, IN: Chase and Shepard.

Woudenberg, Emily (1980). Letter to editor of "The Exchange."

Zanger, Jules (1954). *Captain Frederick Marryat's diary in America*. Ann Arbor, MI: University Microfilms.

Chapter 12

Dvorak, John C. (1987). Origins of the word "nerd." *PC Magazine,* May 26, p. 91.

Geisel, Theodore Seuss (1950). *If I ran the zoo*. New York: Random House.

Rettig, James (1991). Letter to the editor of "The Exchange."

Barnhart, Clarence L., Sol Steinmetz, and Robert K. Barnhart, eds. (1980). *Second Barnhart dictionary of new English*. Bronxville, NY: Barnhart Books.

Seiler, Lauren, and Thomas Suprenant (1991). When we get the libraries we want, will we want the libraries we get? *Wilson Library Bulletin,* June, 65:29+.

Chapter 13

Anderson, Charles R. (1994). "The Exchange." *RQ,* Winter 34:142.

Andrews, Mary Raymond Shipman (1922). *Yellow butterflies*. New York: Charles Scribner's Sons.

Bails, Jerry (1969). *The collector's guide: The first heroic age*. Book is self published. Detroit, MI: J. G. Bails.

Benét, Mrs. Stephen Vincent (1960). Letter to the editor. *The New York Times Book Review,* July 3, p. 19.

Benét, William Rose (1987). *Benét's reader's encyclopedia*. Third edition. New York: Harper & Row.

The century dictionary and cyclopedia (1906). New York: Century Co.

Chattanooga Times (Tennessee). (1939). October 23.

Dahl, Roald (1953). Edward the conqueror. *The New Yorker,* October 31, pp. 28-36.

_____. (1960). *Kiss, kiss*. New York: Knopf.

Davis, Douglas M., ed. (1967). *The world of black humor.* New York: Dutton.

Duke, Neville, and Edward Lanchbery, eds. (1964). *The crowded sky: An anthology of flight from the beginnings of flight to the age of the guided missile.* London: Transworld Publishers, p. 148.

Eadie, John (1876). *The English Bible.* Volume 2. London: Macmillan.

Eliade, Mircea (1987). *The encyclopedia of religion.* Volume 2. New York: Macmillan, p. 55.

Fairy tales and other stories (1929). Cleveland, OH: World Syndicate.

Falwell, Jerry (1980). *Before it's too late.* Garden City, NY: Doubleday, p. 153.

Friedman, Bruce Jay (1965). Those clowns of conscience. *Book Week,* July 18, p. 2.

Gardner, Martin (1977). Mathematical games. *Scientific American,* February, 236: 121-126.

Goodspeed, Edgar J. (1939). *The story of the Apocrypha.* Chicago: University of Chicago Press, p. 7.

Gormley, Myra (1987). A name's biblical beginnings. *Orlando Sentinel,* May 17.

Greenslade, S.L. (1963). *Cambridge history of the Bible.* Volume 3. Cambridge: Cambridge University Press.

Grider, John McGavock (1926). *War birds.* New York: G.H. Doran & Co.

Hassan, Ihab (1964). Laughter in the dark: The new voice in American fiction. *American Scholar,* Autumn, 33:636-668.

Hastings, James (1951). *Encyclopedia of religion and ethics.* Volume VIII. New York: Scribner.

Hawthorn, Horace Boies (1926). *The sociology of rural life.* New York: Century Co.

Helgesen, Martin (1991). Letter to the editor of "The Exchange," July 27.

Jeremiah, David (1982). *Before it's too late.* Nashville, TN: T. Nelson.

Johnston, Ray (1992). *Developing student leaders.* Cajon, CA: Youth Specialities.

King, Marion (1954). *Books and people; Five decades of New York's oldest library.* New York: Macmillan.

Koontz, Dean (2001). *The book of counted sorrows.* Barnes & Noble Digital. Published online only: <http://ebooks.barnesandnoble.com>.

Mackey (1946). *An encyclopedia of Freemasonry.* Revised edition. Chicago: Masonic History Co.

McDevitt, Jean (1950). *Mr. Apple's family.* New York: Doubleday.

Miller, Marjorie (1982). Letter to the editor of "The Exchange."

Morse, J. Mitchell (1965). Madison avenue medicine man [book review]. *Nation,* December 13, p. 475.

Nathan, Robert (1960). *The Weans.* New York: Alfred A. Knopf.

O'Neal, Cothburn (1954). *Dark lady.* New York: Crown.

Perec, Georges (1969). *La Disparition.* Paris: Les Lettres Nouvelles.

Price, Ira Maurice (1956). *Ancestry of our English Bible.* Third edition. New York: Harper & Row.

Ruber, Johannes (1956). *Bach and the heavenly choir.* Translated by Maurice Michael. New York: McGraw-Hill.

_____. (1973). *Die heiligsprechung des Johann Sebastian Bach*. Schwieberdingen: G. Rüber.

Scholes, Robert (1967). *The fabulators*. New York: Oxford University Press, Ch. 3, pt. 1, pp. 35-46.

Smith, H. Allen (1956). *Write me a poem, baby*. New York: Stein and Day, p. 73.

Taylor, Sharon (1989). Letter to the editor of "The Exchange."

Thurber, James (1957). *The Thurber carnival*. New York: Modern Library.

Thurber, James, and E.B. White (1929). *Is sex necessary?* New York: Harper.

Ungerer, Tomi (1971). *I am Papa Snap and these are my favorite no such stories*. New York: Harper.

Vikis-Freibergs, Vaira, ed. (1989). *The linguistics and poetics of Latvian folksongs: Essays in honour of the sesquicentennial of the birth of Kr. Barons*. Kingston, ON: McGill/Queen's University Press.

Walsh, William S. (1914). *Heroes and heroines of fiction: Modern prose and poetry*. Philadelphia, PA: J. B. Lippincott, p. 319.

Wein, Len (1986). *Who's who: The definitive directory of the DC universe*. March, p. 26.

Wiggin, Kate Douglas (1895). *Timothy's quest: A story for anybody, young or old, who cares to read it*. Boston, MA: Houghton Mifflin.

Woods, Ralph L. (1942). *A treasury of the familiar*. New York: Macmillan.

Wright, Ernest Vincent (1939). *Gadsby: A story of over 50,000 words without using the letter e*. Los Angeles: Wetzel Publishing Co.

Zinsser, William K. (1966). "American humor, 1966." *Horizon,* Spring, 8:116-120.

Chapter 15

Adams, Cecil (1988). *More of the straight dope*. New York: Ballantine Books.

Anderla, Georges (1974). *The growth of scientific and technical information, a challenge: Lecture and seminar proceedings*. Washington, DC: National Science Foundation, Office of Science Information Service.

Anderson, Charles (1983). "The Exchange," *RQ,* Summer, 22:239.

Annual report of the director of the mint (1982). Washington, DC: Government Printing Office.

Aradi, Zsolt (1954). *Shrines to our lady around the world*. New York: Farrar.

Astronomical almanac (1982). Washington, DC: Government Publishing Office.

Attwater, Donald (1956). *A dictionary of Mary*. New York: Macmillan, p. 32.

Ball, Oona H. (1932). *Dalmatia*. London: Faber & Faber, pp. 81-82.

Bender, Helen, and Eugene Zepp (1995). Letter to the editor of "The Exchange."

Boldrick, Sam (1995). Letter to the editor of "The Exchange."

Bopp, Bernard (1979). [Department of Physics and Astronomy, University of Toledo], Letter to the editor of "The Exchange."

Boucher, Anthony, ed. (n.d.). *The best from F & SF: Series 5*. Garden City, NY: Doubleday & Co.

Butler, John K. Jr. (1995). Behaviors, trust, and goal achievement in a win-win negotiating role play. *Group and Organization Management,* December, 320: 4:486+.

Catholic almanac (annual). Huntington, IN: Our Sunday Visitor, Inc.

Commins, Dorothy Berliner (1967). *Lullabies of the world.* New York: Random House, pp. xi-xii.

Deedy, John (n.d.). *The Catholic fact book.* Chicago: Thomas More Press, p. 271.

Encyclopedia Britannica (1910). Volume 16. Chicago: Encyclopedia Britannica, p. 54.

Engels, Friedrich (1883). Speech at the graveside of Karl Marx. Highgate Cemetery, London, March 17.

Englund, Ellen (1984). Letter to the editor of "The Exchange."

Evans, Webster (1974). *Encyclopedia of golf.* New York: St. Martins, p. 91.

Evatt, Jay (1995). Letter to the editor of "The Exchange."

Evening Observer (1970). Dunkirk, NY, March.

Fitzpatrick, Kelly (1975). Letter to the editor of "The Exchange."

Folkhart, Burt A. (1994). Master horror writer Robert Bloch dies. *Los Angeles Times,* September 25, Sec. B, p. 4.

Gollman, Robert H. (1981). *Edward Gein: America's most bizarre murderer.* Delavan, WI: Hallberg.

Gordon, Lesley (1977). *Green magic: Flowers, plants and herbs in lore and legend.* New York: Viking.

Greer, Lanier C. (1962). Letter to the *Nation,* June 23, 1962.

Grzimek's animal life encyclopedia (1972). New York: Van Nostrand, Reinhold, 8:218.

Helgesen, Martin (1991). Letter to the editor of "The Exchange."

Holton, Gerald (1971). *Peace News,* June 2.

Hoppel, Joe (1983). *The Sporting News baseball trivia book.* St. Louis, MO: Sporting News Pub. Co.

Houston Chronicle (1920).

Hunter, Jack (1983). [Author of *The Blue Max*]. Telephone conversation with librarian at Illinois State Library.

Israel, Fred, ed. (1968). *Sears, Roebuck Catalogue.* New York: Chelsea House.

Jennings, Ray (1991). On the tracks of the old west. *American Baptist Quarterly,* 10:57-67.

Jones, Jeffrey D. (1991). Chapel cars of the northwest. *American Baptist Quarterly,* 10:7-21.

Kaufman, William I. (1966). *The tea cookbook.* Garden City, NY: Doubleday.

Lewicki, R. J. et al. (1988). *Experiences in management and organizational behavior.* Third edition. New York: Wiley.

Marshall Cavendish illustrated encyclopedia of World War II (1985). New York: Marshall Cavendish.

McCombs, Don, and Fred L. Worth (1983). *World War II super facts*. New York: Warner Books.

McKeon, Jacquie (1975). *If that don't beat the devil: The story of the American Baptist chapel cars*. Self-published, available from Norwegian Bay Books and Gifts, W 2511 Hwy 23, Green Lake, WI 54941.

Mouret, Jean Joseph (n.d.). *Suite de symphonie, No. 1*. Nonesuch H-71009.

Neilson, Francis (1933). *The eleventh commandment*. New York: Viking.

Official rules and record book (1980). Billiard Congress of American, pp. 90-91.

Pasquier, Alain (1975). [Conservator in the Department of Antiquities, Greek and Roman, Louvre Museum], Letter.

Pei, Mario (1965). *The story of language*. Philadelphia, PA: Lippincott, p. 113.

Peterson, Sonia (1990). Letter to the editor of "The Exchange."

Phelps, G. (1976). Family life. *Sign and Sound,* 45:84-85.

Popular Mechanics (1970). Bumper pool table. January, p. 194.

Provine, R.R. (1996). Contagious yawning and laughter: Significance for sensory feature detection, motor pattern generation, imitation, and the evolution of social behavior. In C. M. Heyes and B. G. Galef, eds., *Social learning in animals: The roots of culture*. New York: Academic Press, pp. 179-208.

Provine, R.R. (n.d.). Yawns, laughs, smiles, tickles, and talking: Naturalistic and laboratory studies of facial action and social communication. In J. A. Russell and J. M. Fernandez Dols, eds., *New directions in the study of facial expression*. Cambridge: Cambridge University Press, pp. 158-175.

Raybould, A. (n.d.). Einsiedeln and the shrine of the black Madonna. *Irish Monthly,* 59:22-26.

Robertson, Patrick (1974). *The book of firsts*. New York: Clarkson N. Potter.

Rudolfsky, Geoffrey (1971). The fashionable body. *Horizon,* Autumn, p. 56.

Sadie, Stanley, ed. (1984). *New Grove encyclopedia of music*. Volume 1. London: Macmillan Press, p. 518.

Santos, Bob (1993). Letter to the editor of "The Exchange."

Scharff, Robert (1973). *Golf Magazine's encyclopedia of golf*. New York: Harper, p. 304.

Schweik, Joanne (1970). Telephone conversation with staff member of *The New Yorker*.

Scilken, Marvin (1995). Letter to the editor of "The Exchange."

Shalleck, Jamie (1972). *Tea*. New York: Viking, p. 117.

Shapiro, Fred R. (1986). Personal communication, quoting Rick Tucker, NATwA archivist. May 4.

Simon and Schuster encyclopedia of World War II (1978). New York: Simon & Schuster.

Smith, Clayton (1991). "Chapel car Emmannuel lives," *American Baptist Quarterly,* 10:68-69.

Stephanie, Countess of Leonyay of Vienna (1892). *Lacroma*. n.p.

Stommel, Henry, and Elizabeth Stommel (1983). *Volcano weather: The story of 1816, the year without a summer*. Newport, RI: Seven Seas.

Strain, Paula M. (1977). Letter to the editor of "The Exchange."

Think of your future (1986). Glenview, IL: Scott Foresman, p. 213.

Trager, James (1970). *The enriched fortified, concentrated foodbook.* New York: Grossman.

Tyckoson, David A. (1980). Letter to the editor of "The Exchange."

TV Guide (1983). November 26, p. 55.

Urdang, Lawrence, ed. (1986). *—Ologies and —isms.* Third edition. Detroit, MI: Gale.

The Washington Star (1958). August 13.

_____. (1959). October 13.

Western Police News (1971). February.

Willard, Leroy (1991). The ministry of colporters and chapel cars in Colorado, Wyoming and Utah. *American Baptist Quarterly,* 10:43-56.

Wilson, Robert Anton (1991). *Cosmic trigger v. II: Down to earth.* Phoenix, AZ: New Falcon.

Chapter 16

Rose, Pamela M., Kristin Stoklosa, and Sharon A. Gray (1998). A focus group approach to assessing technostress at the reference desk. *RUSQ* 37:311-317.

Chapter 17

Shipps, Anthony (1990). *The quote sleuth: A manual for the tracer of lost quotations.* Urbana and Chicago: University of Illinois Press.

Conclusion

Hathorn, Clay (1997). The librarian is dead, long live the librarian. *Pre-Text Magazine,* October, <http://www.pretext.com/ oct97/features/story4.htm>.

Penniman, W. David (1992). Walking your talk: Why information managers are not high-tech. In F.W. Lancaster and Linda C. Smith, eds. *Artificial intelligence and expert systems: Will they change the library?* Urbana, IL: University of Illinois, p. 267.

Appendix

RASD (1985). The idea for this survey article was originally developed by Judith B. Quinlan, former chair of the RASD Bibliography Committee. Members of the committee were Lizabeth A. Wilson, assistant undergraduate librarian, University of Illinois at Urbana-Champaign, Chair; Larayne J. Dallas, technical services librarian, Douglas Library, Rutgers University; Kevin Carey, assistant reference librarian, University of Illinois at Chicago; Danise G. Hoover, government documents librarian, Herbert H. Lehman College of the City University of New York; Noelene P. Martin, head, interlibrary loan, Pennsylvania State University; Marion L. Mullen, head of reference, Syracuse University; and David M. Pilachowski, assistant university librarian for public services, Colgate University.

Index

Note: This index includes popular sayings and phrases, titles and lines from poems, songs, and orations, and persons, subjects, and keywords.